THE HOUSE
OF BLUE LEAVES

A N D   T W O   O T H E R   P L A Y S :

LANDSCAPE OF THE BODY
BOSOMS AND NEGLECT

JOHN GUARE

With a New Preface by the Playwright

A PLUME BOOK

NAL PENGUIN INC.

NEW YORK AND SCARBOROUGH, ONTARIO

SIGNET, SIGNET CLASSIC, MENTOR, ONYX, PLUME, MERIDIAN and NAL BOOKS
are published *in the United States* by NAL Penguin Inc.,
1633 Broadway, New York, New York 10019,
in Canada by The New American Library of Canada Limited,
81 Mack Avenue, Scarborough, Ontario M1L 1M8

Library of Congress Cataloging-in-Publication Data
Guare, John.
    The house of blue leaves and two other plays.
    Originally published: Three exposures. San Diego : Harcourt Brace Jovanovich, 1982 or 1983.
    Contents: The house of blue leaves—Landscape of the body—Bosoms and neglect.
    I. Guare, John.   House of blue leaves.   1987.
II. Guare, John.   Landscape of the body.   1987.
III. Guare, John.   Bosoms and neglect.   1987.   IV. Title.
PS3557.U2A6   1987   812'.54   86-33120
ISBN 0-452-25940-1 (pbk.)

First Plume Printing, March, 1987
1   2   3   4   5   6   7   8   9

PRINTED IN THE UNITED STATES OF AMERICA

JOHN GUARE has received a Tony, two Obies, two New York Drama
Critics Circle Awards (best musical—*Two Gentlemen of Verona*—and
best American play), and the New York, Los Angeles, and National
Film Critics Circle Awards for screenplay writing. He was given the
Award of Merit by the American Academy and Institute of Arts and
Letters. He is a Fellow of the New York Institute for the Humanities
and a member of the council of the Dramatists Guild. Mr. Guare lives
in New York.

CONTENTS

PREFACE TO THE PLUME EDITION

In 1904, William Dean Howells wrote to Mark Twain: "You always bewilder by your veracity and I fancy you may tell the truth about yourself. But *all* of it? The Black Truth which we all know of ourselves, in our hearts, not only the whitey brown of the pericardium, or the nice whitened truth of the shirt front? Even you won't tell the Black heart's-truth."

In what tone of voice did he deliver the last phrase to his friend? Accusingly? Threateningly?

A couple of weeks ago, a killer on Death Row in Texas is reported as saying: "I don't think it's fair being executed for a crime you can't remember committing."

Is that what happens to the Black heart's-truth?

By coincidence, the three plays in this book played concurrently in New York City in the spring of 1986. You don't like to go back over your work. You want to keep moving on. The most important play is always the next play. But here was a good part of my working life available between Perry Street and Lincoln Center.

The House of Blue Leaves had opened at the Lincoln Center Theater, *Bosoms and Neglect* at the New York Theater

Workshop, and *Landscape of the Body* at the Cubiculo in the West Fifties.

A group of very recent graduates from Brown University had done the only thing you can do when you are a new actor in New York—they started their own theater company. Their first New York production that spring was *Landscape of the Body*. The people in *Landscape of the Body* are either fourteen or in their early thirties. It was quite eerie seeing the play performed by talented twenty-year-olds who gave the effect of being either very old children or very young adults. They were all intuitive and talented enough to trust the narrative line of the play, and they found, in their way, all the emotional intentions of the piece. But the part of the play that leapt out at me was the scene of the kids in the diner, their thin arms thick with wristwatches they'd collected in sinister ways.

This image had indeed initiated the writing of the play. I had seen kids like these in a booth at a coffee shop on Hudson Street, the boys' arms filled with wristwatches, black, gold, silver, whispering delightedly to the girls, who kept snapping at the bands, dials, faces. Where had the boys got these watches? I mean, they had a *lot* of watches. I went home and wrote out what I thought they might be saying. Years later, in 1986, I felt my own arms filled with my own wristwatches: not sinister, but mysterious as time, and not the new quartz type you throw away, but the kind you've got to keep winding, watches you want to repair.

The House of Blue Leaves has the most wristwatches.

We performed the first act in August 1966 at the Eugene O'Neill Theater Center in Waterford, Connecticut. The completed play finally opened in New York on February 10, 1971. On December 2, 1971, I went to bed winding wristwatches of hubris. The night before, *Two Gentlemen of Verona,* the musical that Mel Shapiro, Galt MacDermot, and I put together, had successfully transferred from Central Park into the St. James Theater. And now I had two shows running in New York—*Blue Leaves* being in the tenth month of its run. At 6 A.M., December 3, 1971, I got a call that the *Blue Leaves* theater had burned. The firemen had put out the flames, then found the set and costumes brutally vandalized, then went to the tenement next door on East 4th Street and found a man with his throat slashed. Subsequent investigation concluded that the fire, the vandalism, and the murder were three separate but overlapping incidents.

So *Blue Leaves* closed. That's the end of that wristwatch.

Slow-motion event: 1981. I leave a Dramatists Guild meeting and round the corner onto Times Square to walk home, and see on the Times Tower, flashing in lights above the Crossroads of the World, the Show Biz Capital of the Universe, the fluorescent neon light bulb wattage blinking at high noon: POPE SHOT. I stop. I count the letters. Again it flashes. Eight little letters—a dopey song runs through my head: "Eight little letters that simply mean—what will this do to my play???"

Writers are all heart.

This pope, at least, was still alive, unlike the previous John Paul, whose sudden death in the seventies after a thirty-day reign produced rumors of murder. My pope had long since died a natural death. My pope had come to New York in 1965 to bring peace to the world. The pope shot today was the Polish pope, the one who had written a play, actually produced in London after he assumed his mantle. (I always wondered what the reviews were like. How do you review a pope? Was this pope already no stranger to assassination attempts?) But I'm there in Times Square, thinking about *The House of Blue Leaves* which, after all, takes place on the day the pope came to New York, and no matter who's playing the part, the pope is still the pope, from Saint Peter on down. And in the play, a boy wants to kill the pope. In 1971, when it opened, people said, "Blow up the pope? Where do you get your ideas?"

The Berkshire Theater Festival in Stockbridge, Massachusetts, was about to begin its 1981 summer season with *The House of Blue Leaves*. My first reaction there in Times Square was a desire to get up to those mountains as soon as possible and see my play, ten years after its opening, in the light of this near-tragic event.

New wristwatch.

Well, the laughter was different.

Before, the audiences had watched the play from a distance. But now, this summertime audience reacted as if a protective glass wall had shattered and tumbled them into the same situation as the people in the play. Was it possible that this proximity of audience to play had made the characters seem even more hungry? Their desperation was the same; the audience's recognition of it was more direct.

Time passes. Some of it Timex. Some of it Mickey Mouse. Some of it Rolex. Some of it Cartier's.

Had Gregory Mosher and Bernard Gersten been so bad in prior lives that they were sentenced to reopen the long-dark Lincoln Center Theater (fondly known as "Loew's Sisyphus")? Instead of issuing a manifesto, they decided to show their commitment to modern American work by opening with a David Mamet bill, and to follow it with a play of mine called *Gardenia,* which Gregory Mosher had directed brilliantly during his tenure at Chicago's Goodman Theater. But the Goodman actors were unavailable. (One, Elizabeth Perkins, because she was doing *Lydia Breeze* at Chicago's Steppenwolf Theater.) Mosher and Gersten elected to put in the second slot *The House of Blue Leaves*.

Stockard Channing was on as Bunny. Jerry Zaks was set

to direct. Swoosie Kurtz came in to see us, assuming there'd been a mistake, that surely we wanted to see her for the part of Bunny, not for Bananas. But Jerry did want her for Bananas. She would win the Tony. As would Jerry. Tony Walton's main problem seemed to be how to design a domestic set for a comedy without making it look like a TV show. He solved it by constructing all of the Borough of Queens under the shadow of the Queensboro Bridge. And Tony would win the Tony. Paul Gallo, the lighting designer, unveiled the set, window by window, store sign by store sign, to the strains of *Also Sprach Zarathustra,* Artie Shaughnessy revealed dreaming in his apartment, buried under the detritus of Nietzsche and Strauss and Queens. A perfect match. Ann Roth costumed what was now a period piece. And with the cast assembled, we went into rehearsal. We threw pennies for luck against the Henry Moore sculpture in the reflecting pool in front of the Lincoln Center Theater.

Opening night: March 19, 1986. Mosher and Gersten ban all reviewers from opening-night celebrations.

We were at The Ginger Man. At 12:45 A.M., I went over to Mike O'Neal, the proprietor (who had given us the opening-night party for the 1971 production and who had driven me back from the original reading in 1966), to see if the damned reviews were out. He came back in about fifteen minutes with a stack of papers. I pulled Gregory Mosher over to the bar. "*You* don't read the reviews. *I* don't read the reviews. But *somebody*'s got to read the reviews." Gregory spread the papers out on the bar, looked them over, closed them. "Raves." He shrugged and went back to the party.

A while later we would go back to The Ginger Man for an important meeting with the cast. Should we move out of the safety of the three-hundred seat Mitzi Newhouse Theater (known as the Minnie Newmouse) and move upstairs into the eleven-hundred seat Vivian Beaumont? Isn't the Beaumont the theater where Quasimodo hangs out in the flies? Is this like one of those horror movies? ("Whatever you do, don't go into the shower!") Chris Walken said, "Go into the shower. People can talk all they want about the Beaumont. Build this. Rebuild that. The Beaumont's got one problem. The seats are too bright red. If you don't fill all the seats up, you can't get a good blackout." Mosher and Gersten looked at each other. They would keep the seats filled.

No one announced the dress rehearsal for the move up to the Beaumont, and yet, at curtain time, over twelve hundred people lined up in front of the theater, past the fountain, over to the State Theater, snaking out onto Ninth Avenue like a dragon at some joyous Chinese festival. Mrs. Pollack, Head Usher since 1965, stood firmly at the entrance: "Thoughts of Noah. Remember the Ark. Two by two. Two by two." John Mahoney began to sing his first song. He got his first laugh. I swear it was like a glacier cracking. That night wasn't a dress rehearsal. It was an exorcism.

I realized that in a sense *The House of Blue Leaves* had never closed.

I think of the wristwatches.

I think of the Black heart's-truth.

The first scene in *Bosoms and Neglect* happened exactly as written, written down in a stupor on the subway ride home immediately after it happened. I did not know where to put this event in my life. The scene hung there. A loud ticking. A while later, the rest of the play ricocheted out of the first scene, imagined, real, confessional, concocted. A play.

On opening night my mother, who for various reasons had never attended the performances of my plays, listened avidly at her home for the reviews. I hadn't known that cameras had recorded the first scene of the play during a preview as the sampling that would accompany the TV reviews. So here is a woman, immersed in a world of fantasy and media, suddenly confronted with the record of a moment in her life she would do anything to flee, coming out of the very instrument of her escape, the TV set.

She had long since taken off her wristwatches.

I had given them back.

And she could never really forgive me.

What happens when you share a Black heart's-truth? I had to pursue mine. She had to flee hers.

In a sense, that's what the plays are. Insurance that the original wound never goes away, that the original crime is never forgiven, is always about to be performed, and is always always in the present tense.

—JOHN GUARE
1986

THE

HOUSE OF

BLUE

LEAVES

———

INTRODUCTION

—

The House of Blue Leaves takes place in Sunnyside, Queens, one of the five boroughs of New York City. You have to understand Queens. It was never a borough with its own identity like Brooklyn that people clapped for on quiz shows if you said you came from there. Brooklyn had been a city before it became part of New York, so it always had its own identity. And the Bronx originally had been Jacob Bronck's farm, which at least gives it something personal, and Staten Island is out there on the way to the sea, and, of course, Manhattan is what people mean when they say New York. Queens was built in the twenties in that flush of optimism as a bedroom community for people on their way up who worked in Manhattan but wanted to pretend they had the better things in life until the inevitable break came and they could make the official move to the Scarsdales and the Ryes and the Greenwiches of their dreams, the pay-off that was the birthright of every American. Queens named its communities Forest Hills, Kew Gardens, Elmhurst, Woodside, Sunnyside, Jackson Heights, Corona, Astoria (after the Astors, of all people). The builders built the apartment houses in mock Tudor or Gothic or Colonial and then named them The Chateau, The El Dorado, Linsley Hall, the Alhambra. We lived first in The East Gate, then moved to The West Gate, then to Hampton Court. And the lobbies had Chippendale furniture and Aztec fireplaces, and the elevators had roman numerals on the buttons.

And in the twenties and thirties and forties you'd move there and move out as soon as you could. Your young married days were over, the promotions came. The ads in the magazines were right. Hallelujah. Queens: a comfortable rest stop, a pleasant rung on the ladder of success, a promise we were promised in some secret dream. (The first paid commercial on American radio was Queensboro Management advertising apartments in Jackson Heights in 1922 on WEAF.) And isn't Manhattan, each day the skyline growing denser and more crenelated, always looming up there in the distance? The elevated subway, the Flushing line, zooms to it, only fourteen minutes from Grand Central Station. Everything you could want you'd find right there in Queens. But the young marrieds become old marrieds, and the children come, but the promotions, the breaks, don't, and you're still there in your bedroom community, your life over the bridge in Manhattan, and the fourteen-minute ride becomes longer every day. Why didn't I get the breaks? I'm right here in the heart of the action, in the bedroom community of the heart of the action, and I live in the El Dorado Apartments and the main street of Jackson Heights has Tudor-topped buildings with pizza slices for sale beneath them and discount radios and discount drugs and discount records and the Chippendale-paneled elevator in my apartment is all carved up with Love To Fuck that no amount of polishing can ever erase. And why do my dreams, which should be the best part of me, why do my dreams, my wants, constantly humiliate me? Why

don't I get the breaks? What happened? I'm hip. I'm hep. I'm
a New Yorker. The heart of the action. Just a subway ride to
the heart of the action. I want to be part of that skyline. I
want to blend into those lights. Hey, dreams, I dreamed you.
I'm not something you curb a dog for. New York is where it
all is. So why aren't I here?

When I was a kid, I wanted to come from Iowa, from
New Mexico, to make the final break and leave, say, the
flatness of Nebraska and get on that Greyhound and get off
that Greyhound at Port Authority and you wave your card-
board suitcase at the sky: I'll Lick You Yet. How do you run
away to your dreams when you're already there? I never
wanted to be any place in my life but New York. How do
you get there when you're there? Fourteen minutes on the
Flushing line is a very long distance. And I guess that's what
this play is about more than anything else: humiliation.
Everyone in the play is constantly being humiliated by their
dreams, their loves, their wants, their best parts. People have
criticized the play for being cruel or unfeeling. I don't think
any play from the Oresteia on down has ever reached the
cruelty of the smallest moments in our lives, what we have
done to others, what others have done to us. I'm not interested so much in how people survive as in how they avoid
humiliation. Chekhov says we must never humiliate one another, and I think avoiding humiliation is the core of tragedy
and comedy and probably of our lives.

This is how the play got written: I went to Saint Joan of
Arc Grammar School in Jackson Heights, Queens, from
1944 to 1952 (wildly pre-Berrigan years). The nuns would
say, If only we could get to Rome, to have His Holiness touch
us, just to see Him, capital H, the Vicar of Christ on Earth—
Vicar, v.i.c.a.r., Vicar, in true spelling-bee style. Oh, dear
God, help me get to Rome, the capital of Italy, and go to that

special little country in the heart of the capital—v.a.t.i.c.a.n.
c.i.t.y.—and touch the Pope. No sisters ever yearned for
Moscow the way those sisters and their pupils yearned for
Rome. And in 1965 I finally got to Rome. Sister Carmela!
Do you hear me? I got here! It's a new Pope, but they're all
the same. Sister Benedict! I'm here! And I looked at the
Rome papers, and there on the front page was a picture of
the Pope. On Queens Boulevard. I got to Rome on the day a
Pope left the Vatican to come to New York for the first
time to plead to the United Nations for peace in the world on
October 4, 1965. He passed through Queens, because you
have to on the way from Kennedy Airport to Manhattan.
Like the Borough of Queens itself, that's how much effect the
Pope's pleas for peace had. The Pope's no loser. Neither is
Artie Shaughnessy, whom *The House of Blue Leaves* is
about. They both have big dreams. Lots of possibilities. The
Pope's just into more real estate.

My parents wrote me about that day that the Pope came
to New York and how thrilled they were, and the letter
caught up with me in Cairo because I was hitching from
Paris to the Sudan. And I started thinking about my parents
and me and why was I in Egypt and what was I doing with
my life and what were they doing with theirs, and that's how
plays get started. The play is autobiographical in the sense
that everything in the play happened in one way or another
over a period of years, and some of it happened in dreams
and some of it could have happened and some of it, luckily,
never happened. But it's autobiographical all the same. My
father worked for the New York Stock Exchange, but he
called it a zoo and Artie in the play is a zoo-keeper. The Billy
in the play is my mother's brother, Billy, a monstrous man
who was head of casting at MGM from the thirties through

the fifties. The Huckleberry Finn episode that begins Act Two is an exact word-for-word reportage of what happened between Billy and me at our first meeting. The play is a blur of many years that pulled together under the umbrella of the Pope's visit.

In 1966 I wrote the first act of the play, and, like some bizarre revenge or disapproval, on the day I finished it my father died. The first act was performed at the O'Neill Theatre Center in Waterford, Connecticut, and I played Artie. The second act came in a rush after that and all the events in that first draft are the same as you'll find in this version. But in 1966 the steam, the impetus for the play, had gone. I wrote another draft of the second act. Another. A fourth. A fifth. A sixth. A director I had been working with was leading the play into abysmal naturalistic areas with all the traps that a set with a kitchen sink in it can have. I was lost on the play until 1969 in London, when one night at the National Theatre I saw Laurence Olivier do *Dance of Death* and the next night, still reeling from it, saw him in Charon's production of *A Flea in Her Ear*. The savage intensity of the first blended into the maniacal intensity of the second, and somewhere in my head *Dance of Death* became the same play as *A Flea in Her Ear*. Why shouldn't Strindberg and Feydeau get married, at least live together, and *The House of Blue Leaves* be their child? For years my two favorite shows had been *Gypsy* and *The Homecoming*. I think the only playwrighting rule is that you have to learn your craft so that you can put on stage plays you would like to see. So I threw away all the second acts of the play, started in again, and, for the first time, understood what I wanted.

Before I was born, just before, my father wrote a song for my mother:

> A stranger's coming to our house.
> I hope he likes us.
> I hope he stays.
> I hope he doesn't go away.

I liked them, loved them, stayed too long, and didn't go away. This play is for them.

—JOHN GUARE

1971

CHARACTERS

Artie Shaughnessy
Ronnie Shaughnessy
Bunny Flingus
Bananas Shaughnessy
Corrinna Stroller
Billy Einhorn
Three nuns
A military policeman
The white man

*A cold apartment in Sunnyside, Queens,
New York City.*

October 4, 1965.

MUSIC AND LYRICS BY JOHN GUARE

Warren Lyons and Betty Ann Besch first presented *The House of Blue Leaves* in New York City on February 10, 1971, at the Truck and Warehouse Theatre. The production was directed by Mel Shapiro.

In 1986, a revival of the play was presented at the Lincoln Center Theater by Gregory Mosher, Director, and Bernard Gersten, Executive Producer. The production opened March 19 at the Mitzi Newhouse Theater. It was directed by Jerry Zaks.

CAST

ARTIE SHAUGHNESSY	*John Mahoney*
RONNIE SHAUGHNESSY	*Ben Stiller*
BUNNY FLINGUS	*Stockard Channing*
BANANAS SHAUGHNESSY	*Swoosie Kurtz*
CORRINNA STROLLER	*Julie Hagerty*
THE HEAD NUN	*Patricia Falkenhain*
THE SECOND NUN	*Jane Cecil*
THE LITTLE NUN	*Ann Talman*
THE MILITARY POLICEMAN	*Ian Blackman*
THE WHITE MAN	*Peter J. Downing*
BILLY EINHORN	*Christopher Walken*

On April 29, 1986, the play transferred to the Vivian Beaumont Theater, and on October 14, 1986 to the Plymouth Theater on 45th Street. Christine Baranski took over the role of Bunny. Jack Wallace played Artie. Patricia Clarkson and Faye Grant played Corrinna. Jack Gwaltney assumed the role of Ronnie. Debra Cole played the Little Nun. The understudies were Brian Evers, Kathleen McKiernan, and Melody Somers. The playwright extends a special salute to Danny Aiello, who became Billy Einhorn.

PROLOGUE

———

The stage of the El Dorado Bar & Grill.

While the house lights are still on, and the audience is still being seated, ARTIE SHAUGHNESSY *comes onstage through the curtains, bows, and sits at the upright piano in front of the curtain. He is forty-five years old. He carries sheet music and an opened bottle of beer. He scowls into the wings and then smiles broadly out front.*

ARTIE, *out front, nervous:* My name is Artie Shaughnessy and I'm going to sing you songs I wrote. I wrote all these songs. Words and the music. Could I have some quiet, please? *He sings brightly:*

> Back together again,
> Back together again.
> Since we split up
> The skies we lit up
> Looked all bit up
> Like Fido chewed them,
> But they're back together again.

You can say you knew us when
We were together
Now we're apart,
Thunder and lightning's
Back in my heart,
And that's the weather to be
When you're back together with me.

Into the wings: Could you please turn the lights down?
A spotlight on me? You promised me a spotlight.
Out front: I got a ballad I'm singing and you promised
me a blue spotlight.

The house lights remain on. People are still finding their seats.

ARTIE *plunges on into a ballad sentimentally:*

I'm looking for Something,
I've searched everywhere,
I'm looking for something
And just when I'm there,
Whenever I'm near it
I can see it and hear it,
I'm almost upon it,
Then it's gone.
It seems I'm looking for Something
But what can it be?
I just need a Someone
To hold close to me.
I'll tell you a secret,
Please keep it entre nous,
That Someone
I thought it was you.

Out front: Could you please take your seats and listen? I'm going to sing you a song I wrote at work today and I hope you like it as much as I do. *He plays and sings:*

> Where is the devil in Evelyn?
> What's it doing in Angela's eyes?
> Evelyn is heavenly,
> Angela's in a devil's disguise.
> I know about the sin in Cynthia
> And the hell in Helen of Troy,
> But where is the devil in Evelyn?
> What's it doing in Angela's eyes?
> Oh boy!
> What's it doing in Angela's eyes?

He leaps up from the piano with his sheet music and beer, bows to the audience. Waits for applause. Bows. Waits. Looks. Runs offstage.

The house lights go down.

ACT ONE

_____

*The living room of a shabby apartment in Sunnyside, Queens.
The room is filled with many lamps and pictures of movie
stars and jungle animals.*

*Upstage center is a bay window, the only window in the
room. Across the opening of the bay is a crisscross-barred
folding gate of the kind jewelers draw across the front of
their stores at night. Outside the window is a fire escape. A
small window in the side of the bay is close enough to the
gate to be opened or closed by reaching through the bars.*

*It's late at night and a street lamp beams some light into
this dark place through the barred window.*

*A piano near the window is covered with hundreds of
pieces of sheet music and manuscript paper and beer bottles.
A jacket, shirt, and pants—the green uniform of a city em-
ployee—are draped over the end of the piano nearest the
window.*

ARTIE *is asleep on the couch, zipped tightly into a sleeping bag, snoring fitfully and mumbling:* Pope Ronnie. Pope
Ronnie. Pope Ronald the First. Pope Ronald.

There is a pullman kitchen with its doors open far stage right.

There are three other doors in the room: a front door with many bolts on it, and two doors that lead to bedrooms.

Even though Artie and his family have lived here eighteen years now, there's still an air of transiency to the room as if they had never unpacked from the time they moved in.

Somebody's at the window, climbing down the fire escape. RONNIE, *Artie's eighteen-year-old son, climbs in the window. He gingerly pulls at the folding gate. It's locked. He stands there for a minute, out of breath.*

He's a young eighteen. His hair is cropped close and he wears big glasses. He wears a heavy army overcoat and under that a suit of army fatigue clothes.

He reaches through the bars to his father's trousers, gets the keys out of the pocket, unlocks the lock, comes into the room and relocks the gate behind him, replaces the pants. He tiptoes past his father, who's still snoring and mumbling: Pope Ronnie. Pope Ronnie. Pope Ronnie.

RONNIE *opens the icebox door, careful not to let the light spill all over the floor. He takes out milk and bread.*

The doorbell buzzes.

ARTIE *groans.*

RONNIE *runs into his bedroom.*

Somebody is knocking on the front door and buzzing quickly, quickly like little mosquito jabs.

ARTIE *stirs. He unzips himself from his sleeping bag, runs to the door. He wears ski pajamas. A key fits into the front door. The door shakes.* ARTIE *undoes the six bolts that hold the door locked. He opens the door, dashes back to his bag, and zips himself in.*

BUNNY FLINGUS *throws open the door. The hall behind her*

*is brilliantly lit. She is a pretty, pink, slightly plump, electric
woman in her late thirties. She wears a fur-collared coat and
plastic booties, and two Brownie cameras on cords clunking
against a pair of binoculars.*

*At the moment she is freezing, uncomfortable, and fur-
ious.*

She storms to the foot of the couch.

BUNNY: You know what your trouble is? You got no sense of
history. You know that? Are you aware of that? Lock
yourself up against history, get drowned by the whole tide
of human events. Sleep it away in your bed. Your bag.
Zip yourself in, Artie. The greatest tide in the history
of the world is coming in today, so don't get your feet wet.

ARTIE, *picking up his glow-in-the-dark alarm:* It's quarter-to-
five in the morning, Bunny—

BUNNY: Lucky for you I got a sense of history. *She sits on the
edge of the couch, picks up the newspaper on the floor.*
You finished last night's? Oooo, it's freezing out there.
Breath's coming out of everybody's mouth like a balloon
in a cartoon. *She rips the paper into long shreds and stuffs
it down into the plastic booties she wears.*

People have been up for hours. Queens Boulevard—
lined for blocks already! Steam coming out of everybody's
mouth! Cripples laid out in the streets in stretchers with
ear muffs on over their bandages. Nuns—you never seen
so many nuns in your life! Ordinary people like you and
me in from New Jersey and Connecticut and there's a
lady even drove in from Ohio—Ohio!—just for today!
She drove four of the most crippled people in Toledo.
They're stretched out in the gutter waiting for the sun to
come out so they can start snapping pictures. I haven't
seen so many people, Artie, so excited since the premiere

of *Cleopatra*. It's that big. Breathe! There's miracles in the
air!

ARTIE: It's soot, Bunny. Polluted air.

BUNNY: All these out-of-staters driving in with cameras and
thermos bottles and you live right here and you're all
zipped in like a turtle. Miss Henshaw, the old lady who's
the check-out girl at the A & P who gyps everybody—her
nephew is a cop and she's saving us two divine places
right by the curb. You're not the only one with connec-
tions. But she can't save them forever. Oh God, Artie,
what a morning! You should see the stars!!! I know all
the stars from the time I worked for that astronomer and
you should see Orion—O'Ryan: the Irish constellation—
I haven't looked up and seen stars in years! I held my
autograph book up and let Jupiter shine on it. Jupiter and
Venus and Mars. They're all out! You got to come see
Orion. He's the hunter and he's pulling his arrow back so
tight in the sky like a Connect-the-Dots picture made up
of all these burning planets. If he ever lets that arrow go,
he'll shoot all the other stars out of the sky—what a welcome for the Pope!

   And right now, the Pope is flying through that star-
filled sky, bumping planets out of the way, and he's asleep
dreaming of the mobs waiting for him. When famous
people go to sleep at night, it's us they dream of, Artie.
The famous ones—they're the real people. We're the crea-
tures of their dreams. You're the dream. I'm the dream.
We have to be there for the Pope's dream. Look at the
light on the Empire State Building swirling around and
around like a burglar's torch looking all through the
sky— Everybody's waiting, Artie—everybody!

ARTIE, *angry:* What I want to know is who the hell is paying
for this wop's trip over here anyway—

BUNNY, *shocked:* Artie! *She reaches through the bars to close the window.* Ssshhh—they'll hear you—

ARTIE: I don't put my nickels and dimes in Sunday collections to pay for any dago holiday—flying over here with his robes and gee-gaws and bringing his buddies over when I can't even afford a trip to Staten Island—

BUNNY, *puzzled:* What's in Staten Island?

ARTIE: Nothing! But I couldn't even afford a nickel ferry-boat ride. I known you two months and can't even afford a present for you—a ring—

BUNNY: I don't need a ring—

ARTIE: At least a friendship ring— *He reaches in his sleeping bag and gets out a cigarette and matches and an ashtray.*

BUNNY, *rubbing his head:* I'd only lose it—

ARTIE, *pulling away:* And this guy's flying over here—not tourist—oh no—

BUNNY, *suspicious of his bitterness:* Where'd you go last night?

ARTIE, *back into his bag:* You go see the Pope. Tell him hello for me.

BUNNY: You went to that amateur night, didn't you—

ARTIE, *signaling toward the other room:* Shut up—she's inside—

BUNNY: You went to the El Dorado Bar Amateur Night, didn't you. I spent two months building you up to be something and you throw yourself away on that drivel—

ARTIE: They talked all the way through it—

BUNNY: Did you play them "Where's the Devil in Evelyn?"?

ARTIE: They talked and walked around all through it—

BUNNY: I wish I'd been there with you. You know what I would've said to them?

To us: The first time I heard "Mairzy Doats" I realized I am listening to a classic. I picked off "Old Black Magic" and "I Could've Danced All Night" as classics the min-

ute I heard them. *She recites:* "Where is the devil in Evelyn? What's it doing in Angela's eyes?" I didn't work in
Macy's Music Department for nix. I know what I'm talking about.
To Artie: That song is a classic. You've written yourself a
classic.

ARTIE: I even had to pay for my own beers.

BUNNY: Pearls before swine. Chalk it up to experience.

ARTIE: The blackboard's getting kind of filled up. I'm too old
to be a young talent.

BUNNY *opens the window through the bars:* Smell the bread—

ARTIE: Shut the window—it's freezing and you're letting all
the dirt in—

BUNNY: Miss Henshaw's saving us this divine place right by
the cemetery so the Pope will have to slow down—

ARTIE: Nothing worse than cold dirt—

The other bedroom door opens and BANANAS SHAUGHNESSY, *a
sick woman in a nightgown, looks at them. They don't see her.*

BUNNY, *ecstatically:* And when he passes by in his limousine,
I'll call out, "Your Holiness, marry us—the hell with peace
to the world—bring peace to us." And he won't hear me
because bands will be playing and the whole city yelling,
but he'll see me because I been eyed by the best of them,
and he'll nod and I'll grab your hand and say, "Marry us,
Pope," and he'll wave his holy hand and all the emeralds
and rubies on his fingers will send Yes beams. In a way,
today's my wedding day. I should have something white
at my throat! Our whole life is beginning—my life—our
life—and we'll be married and go out to California and
Billy will help you. You'll be out there with the big shots—
out where you belong—not in any amateur nights in bars

on Queens Boulevard. Billy will get your songs in movies.
It's not too late to start. With me behind you! Oh, Artie,
the El Dorado Bar will stick up a huge neon sign flashing
onto Queens Boulevard in a couple of years flashing
"Artie Shaughnessy Got Started Here." And nobody'll believe it. Oh, Artie, tables turn.

BANANAS *closes the door.*
ARTIE *gets out of his bag. He sings thoughtfully:*

> Bridges are for burning
> Tables are for turning—

*He turns on all the lights. He pulls Bunny by the pudgy arm
over to the kitchen.*

ARTIE: I'll go see the Pope—
BUNNY, *hugging him:* Oh, I love you!
ARTIE: I'll come if—
BUNNY: You said you'll come. That is tantamount to a promise.
ARTIE: I will if—
BUNNY: Tantamount. Tantamount. You hear that? I didn't
    work in a law office for nix. I could sue you for breach.
ARTIE, *seductively:* Bunny?
BUNNY, *near tears:* I know what you're going to say—
ARTIE, *opening a ketchup bottle under her nose:* Cook for me?
BUNNY, *in a passionate heat:* I knew it. I knew it.
ARTIE: Just breakfast.
BUNNY: You bend my arm and twist my heart but I got to be
    strong.
ARTIE: I'm not asking any ten-course dinner.

To get away from his plea, BUNNY *runs over to the piano, where his clothes are draped.*

BUNNY: Just put your clothes on over the ski p.j.'s I bought you. It's thirty-eight degrees and I don't want you getting your pneumonia back—

ARTIE, *holding up two eggs:* Eggs, baby. Eggs right here.

BUNNY, *holding out his jingling trousers:* Rinse your mouth out to freshen up and come on let's go?

ARTIE, *seductively:* You boil the eggs and pour lemon sauce over—

BUNNY, *shaking the trousers at him:* Hollandaise. I know hollandaise. *She plops down with the weight of the temptation, glum.* It's really cold out, so dress warm— Look, I stuffed the *New York Post* in my booties—plastic just ain't as warm as it used to be.

ARTIE: And you pour the hollandaise over the eggs on English muffins—and then you put the grilled ham on top— I'm making a scrapbook of all the foods you tell me you know how to cook and then I go through the magazines and cut out pictures of what it must look like. *He gets the scrapbook.* Look—veal parmagina—eggplant meringue.

BUNNY: I cooked that for me last night. It was so good I almost died.

ARTIE *sings, as Bunny takes the book and looks through it with great despair:*

> If you cooked my words
> Like they was veal
> I'd say I love you
> For every meal.
> Take my words,

> Garlic and oil them,
> Butter and broil them,
> Sauté and boil them—
> Bunny, let me eat you!

He speaks: Cook for me?

BUNNY: Not till after we're married.

ARTIE: You couldn't give me a little sample right now?

BUNNY: I'm not that kind of girl. I'll sleep with you anytime you want. Anywhere. In two months I've known you, did I refuse you once? Not once! You want me to climb in the bag with you now? Unzip it—go on—unzip it— Give your fingers a smack and I'm flat on my back. I'll sew those words into a sampler for you in our new home in California. We'll hang it right by the front door. Because, Artie, I'm a rotten lay and I know it and you know it and everybody knows it—

ARTIE: What do you mean? Everybody knows it—

BUNNY: I'm not good in bed. It's no insult. I took that sex test in the *Reader's Digest* two weeks ago and I scored twelve. Twelve, Artie! I ran out of that dentist office with tears gushing out of my face. But I face up to the truth about myself. So if I cooked for you now and said I won't sleep with you till we're married, you'd look forward to sleeping with me so much that by the time we did get to that motel near Hollywood, I'd be such a disappointment, you'd never forgive me. My cooking is the only thing I got to lure you on with and hold you with. Artie, we got to keep some magic for the honeymoon. It's my first honeymoon and I want it to be so good, I'm aiming for two million calories. I want to cook for you so bad I walk by the A & P, I get all hot jabs of chili powder inside my thighs ... but I can't till we get those tickets to California

safe in my purse, till Billy knows we're coming, till I got
that ring right on my cooking finger. . . . Don't tempt me
. . . I love you . . .

ARTIE, *beaten:* Two eggs easy over?

BUNNY *shakes her head No:* And I'm sorry last night went
sour . . .

ARTIE *sits down, depressed:* They made me buy my own
beers . . .

BANANAS, *calling from the bedroom:* Is it light? Is it daytime
already?

ARTIE *and* BUNNY *look at each other.*

BUNNY: I'll pour you cornflakes.

ARTIE, *nervous:* You better leave.

BUNNY, *standing her ground:* A nice bowlful?

ARTIE: I don't want her to know yet.

BUNNY: It'll be like a coming attraction.

ARTIE, *pushing her into the kitchen:* You're a tease, Bunny,
and that's the worst thing to be. *He puts on his green shirt
and pants over his pajamas.*

BANANAS *comes out of the bedroom. She's lived in her nightgown for the last six months. She's in her early forties and has
been crying for as long as she's had her nightgown on. She
walks uncertainly, as if hidden barriers lay scattered in her
path.*

BANANAS: Is it morning?

ARTIE, *not knowing how to cope wth her:* Go back to bed.

BANANAS: You're dressed and it's so dark. Did you get an emergency call? Did the lion have babies yet?

ARTIE, *checking that the gate is locked:* The lioness hasn't dropped yet. The jaguar and the cheetah both still waiting. The birds still on their eggs.

BANANAS: Are you leaving to get away from me? Tell me? The truth? You hate me. You hate my looks—my face— my clothes—you hate me. You wish I was fatter so there'd be more of me to hate. You hate me. Don't say that! You love me. I know you love me. You love me. Well, I don't love you. How does that grab you? *She is shaking violently.*

ARTIE *takes pills from the piano and holds her, forcing the pills in her mouth. He's accepted this as one of the natural facts of his life. There is no violence in the action. Her body shakes. The spasms stop. She's quiet for a long time. He walks over to the kitchen.* BUNNY *kisses the palm of his hand.*

BANANAS: For once could you let my emotions come out? If I laugh, you give me a pill. If I cry, you give me a pill . . . no more pills . . . I'm quiet now. . . .

ARTIE *comes out of the kitchen and pours two pills into his hand. He doesn't like to do this.*

BANANAS *smiles:* No! No more—look at me—I'm a peaceful forest, but I can feel all the animals have gone back into hiding and now I'm very quiet. All the wild animals have gone back into hiding. But once—once let me have an emotion? Let the animals come out? I don't like being still, Artie. It makes me afraid . . .

    Brightly: How are you this morning? Sleep well? You were out late last night. I heard you come in and moved over in the bed. Go back to bed and rest. It's still early . . . come back to bed . . .

ARTIE, *finishing dressing:* The Pope is coming today and I'm
  going to see him.

BANANAS: The Pope is coming here?

ARTIE: Yes, he's coming here. We're going to kick off our shoes
  and have a few beers and kick the piano around. *Gently,
  as if to a child:* The Pope is talking to the UN about Vietnam. He's coming over to stop the war so Ronnie won't
  have to go to Vietnam.

BANANAS: Three weeks he's been gone. How can twenty-one
  days be a hundred years?

ARTIE, *to the audience:* This woman doesn't understand. My
  kid is charmed. He gets greetings to go to basic training
  for Vietnam and the Pope does something never done
  before. He flies out of Italy for the first time *ever* to stop
  the war. Ronnie'll be home before you can say Jake Ra-
  binowitz. Ronnie—what a kid—a charmed life ...

BANANAS: I can't go out of the house ... my fingernails are all
  different lengths. I couldn't leave the house. . . . Look—I
  cut this one just yesterday and look how long it is
  already ... but this one ... I cut it months ago right down
  to the quick and it hasn't moved that much. I don't
  understand that. . . . I couldn't see the Pope. I'd embarrass him. My nails are all different. I can feel them
  growing ... they're connected to my veins and heart and
  pulling my insides out my fingers. *She is getting hysterical.*

ARTIE *forces pills down her mouth. She's quiet. She smiles at
  him. Artie's exhausted, upset. He paces up and down in front
  of her, loathing her.*

ARTIE: The Pope takes one look at you standing on Queens
  Boulevard, he'll make the biggest U-turn you ever saw

right back to Rome. *Angry:* I dreamed last night Ronnie
was the Pope and he came today and all the streets were
lined with everybody waiting to meet him—and I felt like
Joseph P. Kennedy, only bigger, because the Pope is a
bigger draw than any President. And it was raining everywhere but on him and when he saw you and me on
Queens Boulevard, he stopped his glass limo and I stepped
into the bubble, but you didn't. He wouldn't take you.

BANANAS: He would take me!

ARTIE, *triumphant:* Your own son denied you. Slammed the
door in your face and you had open-toe shoes on and the
water ran in the heels and out the toes like two Rin Tin
Tins taking a leak—and Ronnie and I drove off to the
UN and the war in Vietnam stopped and he took me back
to Rome and canonized me—made me a Saint of the
Church and in charge of writing all the hymns for the
Church. A hymn couldn't be played unless it was mine
and the whole congregation sang "Where Is the Devil in
Evelyn?" but they made it sound like monks singing it—
You weren't invited, Bananas. Ronnie loved only me. . . .
*He finds himself in front of the kitchen. He smiles at
Bunny.* What a dream . . . it's awful to have to wake up.
For my dreams, I need a passport and shots. I travel the
whole world.

BUNNY, *whispering:* I dreamed once I met Abraham Lincoln.

ARTIE: Did you like him?

BUNNY: He was all right. *She opens a jar of pickles and begins
eating them.*

BANANAS *sees Bunny's fur coat by Ronnie's room. She opens the
front door and throws the coat into the hall. She closes the door
behind her.*

BANANAS: You know what I dream? I dream I'm just waking up and I roam around the house all day crying because of the way my life turned out. And then I do wake up and what do I do? Roam around the house all day crying about the way my life turned out.

An idea comes to ARTIE. *He goes to the piano and sings:*

> The day that the Pope came to New York
> The day that the Pope came to New York,
> It really was comical,
> The Pope wore a yarmulke
> The day that the Pope came to New York.

BANANAS: Don't be disrespectful.

She gets up to go to the kitchen. ARTIE *rushes in front of her and blocks her way.* BUNNY *pushes herself against the icebox trying to hide; she's eating a bowl of cornflakes.*

ARTIE: Stay out of the kitchen. I'll get your food—
BANANAS: Chop it up in small pieces . . .
BUNNY, *in a loud, fierce whisper:* Miss Henshaw cannot reserve our places indefinitely. Tantamount to theft is holding a place other people could use. Tantamount. Her nephew the cop could lock us right up. Make her go back to bed.

ARTIE *fixes Bananas's food on a plate.*
BANANAS *sits up on her haunches and puts her hands, palm downward, under her chin.*

BANANAS: Hello, Artie!

ARTIE: You're going to eat like a human being.

BANANAS: Woof? Woof?

ARTIE: Work all day in a zoo. Come home to a zoo.

He takes a deep breath. He throws her the food. She catches it in her mouth. She rolls on her back.

BANANAS: I like being animals. You know why? I never heard of a famous animal. Oh, a couple of Lassies—an occasional Trigger—but, by and large, animals weren't meant to be famous.

ARTIE *storms into the kitchen.*

BUNNY: What a work of art is a dog. How noble in its thought —how gentle in its dignity—

ARTIE *buries his head against the icebox.*

BANANAS, *smiling out front:* Hello. I haven't had a chance to welcome you. This is my home and I'm your hostess and I should welcome you. I wanted to say Hello and I'm glad you could come. I was very sick a few months ago. I tried to slash my wrists with spoons. But I'm better now and glad to see people. In the house. I couldn't go out. Not yet. Hello. *She walks the length of the stage, smiling at the audience, at us. She has a beautiful smile.*

BUNNY *comes out of the kitchen down to the edge of the stage.*

BUNNY, *to us:* You know what my wish is? The priest told us last Sunday to make a wish when the Pope rides by.

When the Pope rides by, the wish in my heart is gonna knock the Pope's eye out. It is braided in tall letters, all my veins and arteries and aortas are braided into the wish that she dies pretty soon. *She goes back to the kitchen.*

BANANAS, *who has put a red mask on her head:* I had a vision —a nightmare—I saw you talking to a terrible fat woman with newspapers for feet—and she was talking about hunters up in the sky and that she was a dream and you were a dream ... *She crosses to the kitchen, pulls the mask down over her eyes, and comes up behind Bunny:* Hah!!!

BUNNY *screams in terror and runs into the living room.*

BUNNY: I am not taking insults from a sick person. A healthy person can call me anything they want. But insults from a sickie—a sicksicksickie—I don't like to be degraded. A sick person has fumes in their head—you release poison fumes and it makes me sick—dizzy—like riding the back of a bus. No wonder Negroes are fighting so hard to be freed, riding in the back of buses all those years. I'm amazed they even got enough strength to stand up straight. . . . Where's my coat? Artie, where's my coat? My binox and my camera? *To Bananas:* What did you do with my coat, Looney Tunes?

ARTIE *has retrieved the coat from the hallway.*

BUNNY: You soiled my coat! This coat is soiled! Arthur, are you dressed warm? Are you coming?

ARTIE, *embarrassed:* Bananas, I'd like to present—I'd like you to meet—this is Bunny Flingus.

BUNNY: You got the ski p.j.'s I bought you on underneath? You used to go around freezing till I met you. I'll teach

you how to dress warm. I didn't work at ski lodges for
nothing. I worked at Aspen.

BANANAS *thinks it over a moment:* I'm glad you're making
friends, Artie. I'm no good for you.

BUNNY, *taking folders out of her purse, to Bananas:* I might
as well give these to you now. Travel folders to Juarez.
It's a simple procedure—you fly down to Mexico—wet-
back lawyer meets you—sign a paper—jet back to little
old N.Y.

ARTIE: Bunny's more than a friend, Bananas.

BUNNY: Play a little music—"South of the Border"—divorce
Meheeco style!—

ARTIE: Would you get out of here, Bunny. I'll take care of this.

BANANAS *sings hysterically, without words, "South of the
Border."*

BUNNY: I didn't work in a travel agency for nix, Arthur.

ARTIE: Bunny!

BUNNY: I know my way around.

BANANAS *stops singing.*

ARTIE, *taking the folders from Bunny:* She can't even go to
the incinerator alone. You're talking about Mexico—

BUNNY: I know these sick wives. I've seen a dozen like you in
movies. I wasn't an usher for nothing. You live in wheel
chairs just to hold your husband and the minute your
husband's out of the room, you're hopped out of your
wheel chair doing the Charleston and making a general
spectacle of yourself. I see right through you. Tell her,
Artie. Tell her what we're going to do.

ARTIE: We're going to California, Bananas.

BUNNY: Bananas! What a name!

BANANAS: A trip would be nice for you . . .

BUNNY: What a banana—

BANANAS: You could see Billy. . . . I couldn't see Billy. . . .
Almost laughing: I can't see anything . . .

ARTIE: Not a trip.

BUNNY: To live. To live forever.

BANANAS: Remember the time we rode up in the elevator with
Bop Hope? He's such a wonderful man.

ARTIE: I didn't tell you this, Bunny. Last week, I rode out to
Long Island. *To Bananas, taking her hand:* You need
help. We—*I* found a nice hosp . . . By the sea . . . by the
beautiful sea . . . It's an old estate and you can walk from
the train station and it was raining and the roads aren't
paved so it's muddy, but by the road where you turn into
the estate, there was a tree with blue leaves in the rain—
I walked under it to get out of the rain and also because
I had never seen a tree with blue leaves and I walked
under the tree and all the leaves flew away in one big
round bunch—just lifted up, leaving a bare tree. Whoosh.
. . . It was birds. Not blue leaves but birds, waiting to go
to Florida or California . . . and all the birds flew to another tree a couple of hundred feet off and that bare tree
blossomed—snap! like that—with all these blue very
quiet leaves. . . . You'll like the place, Bananas. I talked
to the doctor. He had a mustache. You like mustaches.
And the Blue Cross will handle a lot of it, so we won't
have to worry about expense. . . . You'll like the place
. . . a lot of famous people have had crackdowns there,
so you'll be running in good company.

BANANAS: Shock treatments?

ARTIE: No. No shock treatments.

BANANAS: You swear?

BUNNY: If she needs them, she'll get them.

ARTIE: I'm handling this my way.

BUNNY: I'm sick of you kowtowing to her. Those poison
fumes that come out of her head make me dizzy—suffering—look at her—what does she know about suffering ...

BANANAS: Did you read in the paper about the bull in Madrid
who fought so well they didn't let him die? They healed
him, let him rest before they put him back in the ring,
again and again and again. I don't like the shock treatments, Artie. At least the concentration camps—I was
reading about them, Artie—they put the people in the
ovens and never took them out—but the shock treatments
—they put you in the oven and then they take you out
and then they put you in and then they take you out ...

BUNNY: Did you read *Modern Screen* two months ago? I am
usually not a reader of film magazines, but the cover on
it reached right up and seduced my eye in the health
club. It was a picture like this—*she clutches her head*—
and it was called "Sandra Dee's Night of Hell." Did you
read that by any happenstance? Of course you wouldn't
read it. You can't see anything. You're ignorant. Not you.
Her. The story told of the night before Sandra Dee was
to make her first movie and her mother said, "Sandra,
do you have everything you need?" And she said—
snapped back, real fresh-like—"Leave me alone, Mother.
I'm a big girl now and don't need any help from you." So
her mother said, "All right, Sandra, but remember I'm
always here." Well, her mother closed the door and
Sandra could not find her hair curlers anywhere and she
was too proud to go to her mom and ask her where they
were—

ARTIE: Bunny, I don't understand.

BUNNY: Shut up, I'm not finished yet—and she tore through the house having to look her best for the set tomorrow because it was her first picture and her hair curlers were nowhere! Finally at four in the A.M., her best friend, Annette Funicello, the former Mouseketeer, came over and took the hair curlers out of her very own hair and gave them to Sandra. Thus ended her night of hell, but she had learned a lesson. Suffering—you don't even know the meaning of suffering. You're a nobody and you suffer like a nobody. I'm taking Artie out of this environment and bringing him to California while Billy can still do him some good. Get Artie's songs—his music—into the movies.

ARTIE: I feel I only got about this much life left in me, Bananas. I got to use it. These are my peak years. I got to take this chance. You stay in your room. You're crying. All the time. Ronnie's gone now. This is not a creative atmosphere. . . . Bananas, I'm too old to be a young talent.

BANANAS: I never stopped you all these years . . .

BUNNY: Be proud to admit it, Artie. You were afraid till I came on the scene. Admit it with pride.

ARTIE: I was never afraid. What're you talking about?

BUNNY: No man takes a job feeding animals in the Central Park Zoo unless he's afraid to deal with humans.

ARTIE: I walk right into the cage! What do you mean?

BUNNY: Arthur, I'm trying to talk to your wife. Bananas, I want to be sincere to you and kind.

ARTIE: I'm not afraid of nothing! Put my hand right in the cage—

BUNNY, *sitting down beside Bananas, speaks to her as to a child:* There's a beautiful book of poems by Robert Graves. I never read the book because the title is so beautiful there's no need to read the book: "Man Does.

Woman Is." Look around this apartment. Look at Artie.
Look at him.

ARTIE, *muttering:* I been with panthers.

BUNNY, *with great kindness:* I've never met your son, but—
no insult to you, Artie—but I don't want to. Man does.
What does Artie do? He plays the piano. He creates.
What are you? What is Bananas? Like he said before
when you said you've been having nightmares. Artie said,
"You been looking in the mirror?" Because that's what
you are, Bananas. Look in the mirror.

ARTIE *is playing the piano*—"Where Is the Devil in Evelyn?"

BUNNY: *Man Does. Woman Is.* I didn't work in a lending
library for nothing.

ARTIE: I got panthers licking out of my hands like goddam
pussycats.

BUNNY: Then why don't you ever call Billy?

ARTIE *stops playing:* I got family obligations.

BANANAS, *at the window:* You could take these bars down.
I'm not going to jump.

BUNNY: You're afraid to call Billy and tell him we're coming
out.

BANANAS, *dreamy:* I'd like to jump out right in front of the
Pope's car.

ARTIE: Panthers lay right on their backs and I tickle their arm-
pits. You call me afraid? Hah!

BANANAS: He'd take me in his arms and bless me.

BUNNY: Then call Billy now.

ARTIE: It's the middle of the night!

BUNNY: It's only two in the morning out there now.

ARTIE: Two in the morning is the middle of the night!

BUNNY: In Hollywood! Come off it, he's probably not even in

yet—they're out there frigging and frugging and swing-
ing and eating and dancing. Since Georgina died, he's
probably got a brace of nude starlets splashing in the pool.

ARTIE: I can't call him. He's probably not even in yet—

BUNNY: I don't even think you know him.

ARTIE: Don't know him!

BUNNY: You've been giving me a line—your best friend—big
Hollywood big shot—you don't even know him—

ARTIE: Best friends stay your best friends precisely because you
don't go calling them in the middle of the night.

BUNNY: You been using him—dangling him over my head—
big Hollywood big-shot friend, just to take advantage of
me—just to get in bed with me— Casting couches! I
heard about them—

ARTIE: That's not true!

BUNNY: And you want me to cook for you! I know the score,
baby. I didn't work in a theatrical furniture store for
nothing!

   She tries to put her coat on to leave. He pulls it off her.
If you can't call your best friends in the middle of the
night, then who can you call—taking advantage of me in
a steam bath—

BANANAS, *picking up the phone:* You want me to get Billy on
the phone?

ARTIE: You stay out of this!

BANANAS: He was always my much better friend than yours,
Artie.

ARTIE: Your friend! Billy and I only went to kindergarten
together, grammar school together, high school together
till his family moved away—Fate always kept an eye out
to keep us friends. *He sings:*

   If you're ever in a jam, here I am.

BANANAS *sings:*

>   Friendship.

ARTIE *sings:*

>   If you're ever up a tree, just phone me.

ARTIE *turns to us exuberantly:* He got stationed making training movies and off each reel there's what they call leader
—undeveloped film—and he started snipping that leader
off, so by the time we all got discharged, he had enough
film spliced up to film Twenty Commandments. He
made his movie right here on the streets of New York
and Rossellini was making his movies in Italy, only Billy
was making them here in America and better. He sold
everything he had and he made *Conduct of Life* and it's
still playing in museums. It's at the Museum of Modern
Art next week—and Twentieth Century–Fox signed him
and MGM signed him—they both signed him to full
contracts—the first time anybody ever got signed by two
studios at once. . . . You only knew him about six months'
worth, Bananas, when he was making the picture. And
everybody in that picture became a star and Billy is still
making great pictures.

BUNNY: In his latest one, will you ever forget that moment
when Doris Day comes down that flight of stairs in that
bathrobe and thinks Rock Hudson is the plumber to fix
her bathtub and in reality he's an atomic scientist.

BANANAS: I didn't see that . . .

ARTIE, *mocking:* Bananas doesn't go out of the house . . .

BUNNY, *stars in her eyes:* Call him, Artie.

ARTIE: He gets up early to be on the set. I don't want to wake him up—

BUNNY: Within the next two years, you could be out there in a black tie waiting for the lady—Greer Garson—to open the envelope and say as the world holds its breath—"And the winner of the Oscar for this year's Best Song is—" *She rips a travel folder very slowly.*

ARTIE, *leaning forward:* Who is it? Who won?

BUNNY: And now Miss Mitzi Gaynor and Mr. Franco Corelli of the Metropolitan Opera will sing the winning song for you from the picture of the same name made by his good friend and genius, Billy Einhorn. The winner is of course Mr. Arthur M. Shaughnessy.

ARTIE *goes to the telephone. He dials once, then:* Operator, I want to call in Bel Air, Los Angeles—

BUNNY: You got the number?

ARTIE: Tattooed, baby. Tattooed. Your heart and his telephone number right on my chest like a sailor. Not you, operator. I want and fast I want in Los Angeles in Bel Air GR 2-4129 and I will not dial it because I want to speak personally to my good friend and genius, Mr. Billy Einhorn . . . E-I-N—don't you know how to spell it? The name of only Hollywood's leading director my friend and you better not give this number to any of your friends and call him up and bother him asking for screen tests.

BUNNY: When I was an operator, they made us take oaths. I had Marlon Brando's number for years and pistols couldn't've dragged it out of my head—they make you raise your right hand—

ARTIE: My number is RA 1-2276 and don't go giving that number away and I want a good connection . . . hang on, Bunny—*she takes his extended hand*—you can hear the beepbeepbeeps—we're traveling across the country—hang on! Ring. It's ringing. Ring.

BUNNY, *his palm and her palm forming one praying hand:* Oh God, please—

ARTIE, *pulling away from her:* Ring. It's up. Hello? Billy? Yes, operator, get off—that's Billy. Will you get off— *To Bunny:* I should've called station-to-station. He picked it right up and everything. Billy! This is Ramon Navarro! ... No, Billy, it's Artie Shaughnessy. Artie. No, New York! Did I wake you up! Can you hear me! Billy, hello. I got to tell you something—first of all, I got to tell you how bad I feel about Georgina dying—the good die young—what can I say—and second, since you, you old bum, never come back to your old stomping grounds—your happy hunting grounds, I'm thinking of coming out to see you. ... I know you can fix up a tour of the studios and that'd be great ... and you can get us hotel reservations—that's just fine. ... But, Billy, I'm thinking I got to get away— not just a vacation—but make a change, get a break, if you know what I'm getting at. ... Bananas is fine. She's right here. We were just thinking about you— NO, IT'S NOT FINE. Billy, this sounds cruel to say but Bananas is as dead for me as Georgina is for you. I'm in love with a remarkable wonderful girl—yeah, she's here too—who I should've married years ago—no, we didn't know her years ago—I only met her two months ago—yeah. ...

Secretively, pulling the phone off to the corner: It's kind of funny, a chimpanzee knocked me in the back and kinked my back out of whack and I went to this health club to work it out and in the steam section with all the steam I got lost and I went into this steam room and there was Bunny—yeah, just towels—I mean you could make a movie out of this, it was so romantic— She couldn't see

me and she started talking about the weight she had to
take off and the food she had to give up and she started
talking about duckling with orange sauce and oysters
baked with spinach and shrimps baked in the juice of
melted sturgeon eyes which caviar comes from—well,
you know me and food and I got so excited and the
steam's getting thicker and thicker and I ripped off my
towel and kind of raped her . . . and she was quiet for a
long time and then she finally said one of the greatest
lines of all time. . . . She said, "There's a man in here." . . .
And she was in her sheet like a toga and I was all toga'd
up and I swear, Billy, we were gods and goddesses and
the steam bubbled up and swirled and it was Mount
Olympus. I'm a new man, Billy—a new man—and I got
to make a start before it's too late and I'm calling you,
crawling on my hands and knees—no, not like that, I'm
standing up straight and talking to my best buddy and
saying Can I come see you and bring Bunny and talk over
old times. . . . I'll pay my own way. I'm not asking you
for nothing. Just your friendship. I think about you so
much and I read about you in the columns and *Conduct
of Life* is playing at the Museum of Modern Art next
week and I get nervous calling you and that Doris Day
pic—well, Bunny and I fell out of our loge seats—no,
Bananas couldn't see it—she don't go out of the house
much. . . . I get nervous about calling you because, well,
you know, and I'm not asking for any Auld Lang Syne
treatment, but it must be kind of lonely with Georgina
gone and we sent five dollars in to the Damon Runyon
Cancer Fund like Walter Winchell said to do and we're
gonna send more and it must be kind of lonely and the
three of us—Bunny and you and me—could have some
laughs. What do you say? You write me and let me

know your schedule and we can come any time. But soon. Okay, buddy? Okay? No, this is my call. I'm paying for this call so you don't have to worry—talking to you I get all opened up. You still drinking rye? Jack Daniels! Set out the glasses—open the bottle—no, I'll bring the bottle—we'll see you soon. Good night, Billy. *The call is over.*

Soon, Billy. Soon. Soon. *He hangs up.*

BUNNY *dances and sings:*

> The day that the Pope came to New York
> The day that the Pope came to New York,
> It really was comical,
> The Pope wore a yarmulke
> The day that the Pope came to New York.

ARTIE, *stunned:* Did you hear me!

BUNNY: You made me sound like the Moon Coming Over the Mountain! So fat!

ARTIE: He said to say hello to you, Bananas.

BANANAS: Hello . . .

ARTIE, *to Bunny:* Get the copy of *Life* magazine with the story on his house . . .

BUNNY *gets the magazine off the top of the piano.*

BUNNY, *thrilled:* You made me sound so fat! So Kate Smith!

ARTIE, *taking the magazine and opening it:* Look at his house— on the highest part of all Los Angeles—

BUNNY, *devouring the pictures:* It's Bel Air! I know Bel Air! I mean, I don't know Bel Air, but I mean, I know Bel Air!

ARTIE *and* BUNNY *flop on the sofa.* BANANAS, *in the kitchen behind them, throws rice at them.*

BUNNY: Let's get out of here. She gives me the weeping willies.

BANANAS: Oh, no, I'm all right. I was just thinking how lucky we all are. You going off to California and me going off to the loony bin—

ARTIE, *correcting her:* It's a rest place—

BANANAS: With beautiful blue trees, huh?

ARTIE: Birds—waiting to go to Florida or California—

BANANAS: Maybe it was a flock of insane bluebirds that got committed—

ARTIE, *to Bunny:* I'm gonna take a shower. My shirt's all damp from the telephone call.

BUNNY, *putting her coat on:* Artie, I'll be at the corner of Forty-sixth Street near the cemetery by the TV repair store. . . . Hello, John the Baptist. That's who you are. John the Baptist. You called Billy and prepared the way— the way for yourself. Oh, Christ, the dinners I'm gonna cook for you. *She sings:*

> It really was comical,
> The Pope wore a yarmulke
> The day that the Pope came to New York.

She blows a kiss and exits.
ARTIE *yelps triumphantly. He comes downstage.*

ARTIE: Hello, Billy. I'm here. I got all my music. *He sings:*

> I'm here with bells on,
> Ringing out how I feel.
> I'll ring,

I'll roar,
I'll sing
Encore!
I'm here with bells on.
Ring! Ring! Ring!

BANANAS, *very depressed:* The people downstairs . . . they'll be
pumping broomsticks on the ceiling . . .

ARTIE, *jubilant:* For once the people downstairs is Bunny! *He
sings:*

For once the people downstairs is Bunny!

He speaks now, jumping up and down on the floor:
Whenever the conversation gets around to something you
don't like, you start ringing bells of concern for the people downstairs. For once in my life, the people downstairs
is Bunny and I am a free man! *He bangs all over the keys
of the piano.* And that's a symphony for the people upstairs!

BANANAS: There's just the roof upstairs . . .

ARTIE: Yeah, and you know roofs well. I give up six months of
my life taking care of you and one morning I wake up
and you're gone and all you got on is a nightgown and
your bare feet—the corns of your bare feet for slippers.
And it's snowing out, snowing a blizzard, and you're out
in it. Twenty-four hours you're gone and the police are up
here and long since gone and you're being broadcasted for
in thirteen states all covered with snow—and I look out
that window and I see a gray smudge in a nightgown
standing on the edge of the roof over there—in a snow-
bank and I'm praying to God and I run out of this place,
across the street. And I grab you down and you're so cold,

your nightgown cuts into me like glass breaking and I carried you back here and you didn't even catch a cold— not even a sniffle. If you had just a sniffle, I could've forgiven you. . . . You just look at me with that dead look you got right now. . . . You stay out twenty-four hours in a blizzard hopping from roof to roof without even a pair of drawers on—and *I* get the pneumonia.

BANANAS: Can I have my song?

ARTIE: You're tone-deaf. *He hits two bad notes on the piano.* Like that.

BANANAS: So I won't sing it. . . . My troubles all began a year ago—two years ago today—two days ago today? Today.

ARTIE *plays "The Anniversary Waltz."*

BANANAS: We used to have a beautiful old green Buick. The Green Latrine! . . . I'm not allowed to drive it any more . . . but when I could drive it . . . the last time I drove it, I drove into Manhattan.

ARTIE *plays "In My Merry Oldsmobile."*

BANANAS: And I drive down Broadway—to the Crossroads of the World.

ARTIE *plays "Forty-second Street."*

BANANAS: I see a scene that you wouldn't see in your wildest dreams. Forty-second Street. Broadway. Four corners. Four people. One on each corner. All waving for taxis. Cardinal Spellman. Jackie Kennedy. Bob Hope. President Johnson. All carrying suitcases. Taxi! Taxi! I stop in the middle of the street—the middle of Broadway—and I get

out of my Green Latrine and yell, "Get in. I'm a gypsy. A
gypsy cab. Get in. I'll take you where you want to go.
Don't you all know each other? Get in! Get in!"

They keep waving for cabs. I run over to President
Johnson and grab him by the arm. "Get in." And pull
Jackie Kennedy into my car and John-John, who I didn't
see, starts crying and Jackie hits me and I hit her and I
grab Bob Hope and push Cardinal Spellman into the back
seat, crying and laughing, "I'll take you where you want to
go. Get in! Give me your suitcases"—and the suitcases spill
open and Jackie Kennedy's wigs blow down Forty-Second
Street and Cardinal Spellman hits me and Johnson
screams and I hit him. I hit them all. And then the Green
Latrine blew four flat tires and sinks and I run to protect
the car and four cabs appear and all my friends run into
four different cabs. And cars are honking at me to move.

I push the car over the bridge back to Queens. You're
asleep. I turn on Johnny Carson to get my mind off and
there's Cardinal Spellman and Bob Hope, whose ski-nose
is still bleeding, and they tell the story of what happened
to them and everybody laughs. Thirty million people
watch Johnny Carson and they all laugh. At me. At me.
I'm nobody. I knew all those people better than me. You.
Ronnie. I know everything about them. Why can't they
love me?

And then it began to snow and I went up on the
roof . . .

ARTIE, *after a long pause:* Come see the Pope. Pray. Miracles
happen. He'll bless you. *Reader's Digest* has an article this
month on how prayer answers things. Pray? Kneel down
in the street? The Pope can cure you. The *Reader's Digest*
don't afford to crap around.

BANANAS: My fingernails are all different lengths. Everybody'd laugh . . .

ARTIE: We used to have fun. Sometimes I miss you so much . . .

BANANAS, *smiling nervously:* If I had gloves to put on my hands . . .

ARTIE: The Pope must be landing now. I'm going to turn on the television. I want you to see him. *He turns on the television.* Here he is. He's getting off the plane. Bananas, look. Look at the screen. *He pulls her to the screen. He makes her kneel in front of it.* Oh God, help Bananas. Please God? Say a prayer, Bananas. Say, "Make me better, God . . ."

BANANAS: Make me better, God . . .

ARTIE: "So Artie can go away in peace." . . . Here's the Pope. *He speaks to the screen.* Get out of the way! Let a sick woman see! There he is! Kiss him? Kiss his hem, Bananas. He'll cure you! Kiss him.

BANANAS *leans forward to kiss the screen. She looks up and laughs at her husband.*

BANANAS: The screen is so cold . . .

ARTIE, *leaping:* Get out of the way, you goddam newsman! *He pushes Bananas aside and kisses the screen.* Help me— help me—Your Holiness . . .

While he hugs the set, BANANAS *leaves the room to go into her bedroom.*

The front door flies open. BUNNY *bursts in, flushed, bubbling. She has an enormous "I Love Paul" button on her coat.*

BUNNY: He's landed! He's landed! It's on everybody's tran-

sistors and you're still here! And the school kids!—the
Pope drives by, he sees all those school kids, he's gonna
come out for birth control today!! Churches will be selling
Holy Diaphragms with pictures of Saint Christopher and
all the saints on them. You mark my words.

To us, indicating her button: They ran out of "Welcome
Pope" buttons so I ran downstairs and got my leftover
from when the Beatles were here! I am famished. What
a day! *She goes to the icebox and downs a bottle of soda.*

BANANAS *comes out of the bedroom. She wears a coat over her
nightgown, and two different shoes, one higher than the
other, and a hat cocked on her head. She is smiling. She
is pulling on gloves.*

ARTIE *turns off the TV.*

BUNNY *gapes. Band music plays joyously in the distance.*

ARTIE *goes to Bananas and takes her arm.*

BUNNY: Now wait one minute. Miss Henshaw is going to be
mighty pissed off.

ARTIE: Just for today.

BANANAS: Hold me tight. . . .

ARTIE, *grabbing his coat:* Over the threshold . . . *They go out.*

BUNNY: Artie, are you dressed warm? Are you dressed warm?
Your music! You forgot your music! You gotta get it
blessed by the Pope!!

BANANAS *appears in the doorway and grabs the music from
Bunny.*

BANANAS *sings:*

It really was comical,
The Pope wore a yarmulke
The day that the Pope came to New York.

BUNNY: You witch! You'll be in Bellevue tonight with enough
   shock treatments they can plug Times Square into your
   ear. I didn't work for Con Edison for nothing! *She storms*
   out after them and slams the door behind her.

The bedroom door RONNIE *went into at the beginning of the*
act opens. He comes out carrying a large gift box.
   He comes downstage and stares at us.

CURTAIN

A C T   T W O

RONNIE *is standing in the same position, staring at us. Out of the pockets of his fatigues he first takes two hand grenades, then wire, then his father's alarm clock. He wires them together, setting the alarm on the clock at a special time. He puts the whole device into the gift box.*

He is very young—looks barely seventeen—his hair is cropped close all over; he is tall, skinny. He speaks with deep, suffocated religious fervor; his eyes bulge with a strange mixture of terrifying innocence and diabolism. You can't figure out whether he'd be a gargoyle on some Gothic cathedral or a skinny cherub on some altar.

RONNIE: My father tell you all about me? Pope Ronnie? Charmed life? How great I am? That's how he is with you. You should hear him with me, you'd sing a different tune pretty quick, and it wouldn't be "Where Is the Devil in Evelyn?"

He goes into his room and returns carrying a large, dusty box.
He opens it and takes out an altar boy's bright red cassock and
white surplice that used to fit him when he was twelve. As
he puts them on, he speaks to us:

I was twelve years old and all the newspapers had headlines on my twelfth birthday that Billy was coming to
town. And *Life* was doing stories on him and *Look* and
the newsreels, because Billy was searching America to
find the Ideal American Boy to play Huckleberry Finn.
And Billy came to New York and called my father and
asked him if he could stay here—Billy needed a hide-out.
In Waldorf-Astorias all over the country, chambermaids
would wheel in silver carts to change the sheets. And out
of the sheets would hop little boys saying, "Hello, I'm
Huckleberry Finn." All over the country, little boys
dressed in blue jeans and straw hats would be sent to him
in crates, be under the silver cover covering his dinner, in
his medicine cabinet in all his hotel rooms, his suitcase—
"Hello, Hello, I'm Huckleberry Finn." And he was coming here to hide out. Here—Billy coming here— I asked
the nun in school who was Huckleberry Finn—
　The nun in Queen of Martyrs knew. She told me. The
Ideal American Boy. And coming home, all the store
windows reflected me and the mirror in the tailor shop
said, "Hello, Huck." The butcher shop window said,
"Hello, Huck. Hello, Huckleberry Finn. All America
Wants to Meet Billy and He'll Be Hiding Out in Your
House." I came home—went in there—into my room and
packed my bag. . . . I knew Billy would see me and take me
back to California with him that very day. This room
smelled of ammonia and air freshener and these slipcovers

were new that day and my parents were filling up the ice-box in their brand-new clothes, filling up the icebox with food and liquor as excited as if the Pope was coming—and nervous because they hadn't seen him in a long while—Billy. They told me my new clothes were on my bed. To go get dressed. I didn't want to tell them I'd be leaving shortly to start a new life. That I'd be flying out to California with Billy on the H.M.S. *Huckleberry*. I didn't want tears from them—only trails of envy. . . . I went to my room and packed my bag and waited.

The doorbell rang. *He starts hitting two notes on the piano.* If you listen close, you can still hear the echoes of those wet kisses and handshakes and tears and backs getting hit and Hello, Billys, Hello. They talked for a long time about people from their past. And then my father called out, "Ronnie, guess who? Billy, we named him after your father. Ronnie, guess who?"

I picked up my bag and said good-bye to myself in the mirror. Came out. Billy there. Smiling.

It suddenly dawned on me. You had to do things to get parts.

I began dancing. And singing. Immediately. Things I have never done in my life—before or since. I stood on my head and skipped and whirled—*he cartwheels across the stage*—spectacular leaps in the air so I could see veins in the ceiling—ran up and down the keys of the piano and sang and began laughing and crying soft and loud to show off all my emotions. And I heard music and drums that I couldn't even keep up with. And then cut off all my emotions just like that. Instantly. And took a deep bow like the Dying Swan I saw on Ed Sullivan. *He bows deeply*. I picked up my suitcase and waited by the door.

Billy turned to my parents, whose jaws were down to about there, and Billy said, "You never told me you had a mentally retarded child."

"You never told me I had an idiot for a godchild," and I picked up my bag and went into my room and shut the door and never came out the whole time he was here.

My only triumph was he could never find a Huckleberry Finn. Another company made the picture a few years later, but it flopped.

My father thinks I'm nothing. Billy. My sergeant. They laugh at me. You laughing at me? I'm going to fool you all. By tonight, I'll be on headlines all over the world. Cover of *Time. Life.* TV specials. *He shows a picture of himself on the wall.* I hope they use this picture of me— I look better with hair— Go ahead—laugh. Because you know what I think of you? *He gives us hesitant Bronx cheers.* I'm sorry you had to hear that—pay popular prices to hear that. But I don't care. I'll show you all. I'll be too big for any of you.

The sound of a key in the door. ARTIE *is heard singing "The Day That the Pope Came to New York."*

RONNIE *exits to his room, carrying the gift box containing the bomb.*

ARTIE *runs in and begins grabbing up sheet music.*

ARTIE: Bunny says, "Arthur, I am not talking to you but I'll say it to the breeze: Arthur, get your music. 'Bring On the Girls.' Hold up your music for when the Pope His Holiness rides by."
To us: You heard these songs. They don't need blessings. I hate to get all kissyass, you know? But it can't hurt.

"Bring On the Girls." Where is it? Whenever Bunny cleans up in here you never can find anything. You should see the two girls holding each other up like two sisters and they're not even speaking which makes them even more like sisters. Wouldn't it be great if they fell in love and we all could stay ...

A beautiful girl in a fur coat stands hesitantly in the doorway. She carries flowers and liquor in her arms. She is CORRINNA STROLLER.

CORRINNA: Mr. Shaughnessy?

ARTIE: Did I win something? Where'd I put those sweepstake tickets—I'll get them—

CORRINNA: Oh oh oh ohhhhh—it's just like Billy said. Oh God, it's like walking into a photo album. Norman Rockwell. Grandma Moses. Let me look at you. Oh, I was afraid with the Pope, you'd be out, but it's just like Billy said. You're here!

ARTIE: Billy? We talked this morning ...

CORRINNA: Billy called me just as I was checking out and told me to stop by on my way to the airport.

ARTIE: A friend of Billy's and you stay in a hotel? Don't you know any friend of Billy's has a permanent address right here. ... Don't tell me ...

CORRINNA: What?

ARTIE: I know your name.

CORRINNA, *very pleased:* Oh, how could you ...

ARTIE: You're Corrinna Stroller.

CORRINNA, *modestly:* Oh ...

ARTIE: I knew it. I saw that one movie you made for Billy ...

CORRINNA: That's how we met.

ARTIE: And then you retired—

CORRINNA—*a sore point:* Well . . .

ARTIE: You were fantastic.

CORRINNA: Well . . .

ARTIE: Why did you quit?

CORRINNA: Well . . .

ARTIE: Will you sit down for a few minutes? Just let me get my girls. If you left without seeing them. . . . *He comes down to us.* You call Billy and he sends stars. Stars! *To Corrinna:* The icebox is yours. I'll be right back. Corrinna Stroller! *He exits.*

CORRINNA *is alone. There is a high, loud whine. Her hands go to her ears. The whine becomes very electronic. The sound is almost painful. She pulls a hearing aid from each ear. The sound suddenly stops. She reaches into her dress and removes a receiver that the aids are wired to.*

She sits on the couch and replaces the dead transistors with fresh transistors. She looks up.

CORRINNA, *to us:* Don't tell—please? I don't want them to know I'm deaf. I don't want them to think Billy's going around with some deaf girl. There was an accident on a set—a set of Billy's. . . . I can hear with my transistors. *She shows us a vial containing new transistors.* I want them to know me first. So please, don't tell. Please.

BUNNY *enters with Artie close behind.*

BUNNY: Where is she? Where is she? Oh—*Corrinna hastily puts her hearing aids away*—Corrinna Stroller! Limos in the streets. Oh, Miss Stroller, I only saw your one movie, *Warmonger*, but it is permanently enshrined in the Loew's of my heart. *To us:* That scene where she blows up in the landmine—so realistic. *To Corrinna:* And then you never made another picture. What happened?

CORRINNA: I just dropped in to say hi—

BUNNY: Hi! Oh, Corrinna Stroller! *To Artie:* You know that phony Mrs. Binard in 4-C who wouldn't give you the time of day—she says, "Oh Miss Flingus, is this limo connected to you?" I'd like to put my fist through her dimple. *She takes the newspapers out of her booties. To Corrinna:* Hi, I'm Bunny, the future His. You want some snacks?

CORRINNA: I've got to catch a plane—

BUNNY: Should I send some down to the chauffeur? Oh, stay, have some snacks—

ARTIE: Are you gonna cook?

BUNNY: Just short-order snacks, while you audition . . .

ARTIE: Audition?

BUNNY: You get your ass on those tunes while the Pope's blessing is still hot on them. Artie, the Pope looked right at me! We're in solid. *To Corrinna, with a tray of celery:* Ta Ta!! That's a trumpet. Look, before we start chattering about hellos and how-are-yous and who we all are and old times and new times, bite into a celery for some quick energy and I'll get you a soda and Arthur here writes songs that could be perfect for Oscar-winning medleys and love themes of important motion-picture presentations and you should tell Billy about it. Artie being the Webster's Dictionary Definition for Mr. Shy. *Gone with the Wind. The Wizard of Oz.* That is the calibre of film that I am talking about. And His Holiness the Very Same Pope has seen these songs and given them his blessings. *She shows the sheet music to Corrinna.*

CORRINNA: I'd love to, but I have a very slight post-nasal drip.

BUNNY: Isn't she wonderful! Go on, Artie, while Mister Magic still shimmers!

ARTIE, *at the piano, sings:*

> Back together again,
> Back together again.

THREE NUNS *appear at the window.*

CORRINNA *sees them and screams. Her transistors fall on the floor.*

CORRINNA: My transistors!! *She is down on her knees, search-for them.*

BUNNY: Get away from here! Scat! Get away! Go! Go!

HEAD NUN: We got locked out on your roof! Please, it's fifty below and our fingers are icicles and our lips are the color of Mary—

SECOND NUN: The doorknob came right off in our hands—

ARTIE: I'm sorry, Sisters, but these are secret auditions . . .

HEAD NUN: But we missed the Pope! And we came all the way from Ridgewood! Let us see it on television!

ALL THREE NUNS: Please! Please! On television!

ARTIE, *opening the gate:* Oh, all right . . .

BUNNY: Don't do it, Arthur. *She sees Corrinna on the floor.* What's the matter, honey, did you drop something? It's like a regular Vatican here.

During the scene CORRINNA *will pick up her transistors at any moment she feels she is not being observed. She keeps them in a small vial for safety.*

The NUNS *are now inside.*

SECOND NUN: We stole Monsignor Boyle's binoculars!

HEAD NUN: We couldn't see the Pope, the crowds were so thick, so we climbed up onto your roof . . .

SECOND NUN: And I put the binoculars up to my eyes and got the Pope in focus and the pressure of Him against my eyes, oh God, the binoculars flew out of my hands like a miracle in reverse . . .

HEAD NUN: We'll be quiet.

LITTLE NUN, *in the kitchen:* Look! Peanut butter! They have peanut butter! *To us:* We're not allowed peanut butter!

ARTIE: Put that away!

HEAD NUN, *a sergeant:* You! Get over here.

The LITTLE NUN *obeys.* ARTIE *turns on the TV.*

SECOND NUN: Oh, color. They don't have color!

HEAD NUN: Would you have some beers? To warm us up? We will pray for you many years for your kindness today.

BANANAS, *offstage, in the hall, terrified:* Artie? Artie, are you there? Is this my home? Artie?

ARTIE: Oh God, Bananas. Bunny, get the beers, would you?

BUNNY: What do I look like?

ARTIE *runs into the hall to retrieve Bananas.*

BUNNY, *to Corrinna:* Excuse the interruption; we're not religious as such, but his heart is the Sistine Chapel. *She goes to the kitchen for beers.*

BANANAS, *entering with Artie:* I didn't know where home was. Miss Henshaw showed me. And then your fat girlfriend ran away. I had to ask directions how to get back.

BUNNY *plunks the beers on the TV set.*

SECOND NUN: Oh, imported! They don't have imported! We
  could've stayed back in Ridgewood and watched color
  and had imported, but no, she's got to see everything in
  the flesh—

HEAD NUN: You were the one who dropped the binoculars—

SECOND NUN: You were the one who stole them—

BANANAS: Artie, did you bring work home from the office?

ARTIE: They're nuns, Bananas, nuns.

HEAD NUN: We got locked out on the upstairs roof. Hi!

BANANAS: Hi!

ARTIE: This is Corrinna Stroller, Billy's girlfriend. Corrinna,
  this is Bananas.

THE NUNS: Corrinna Stroller! The movie star!

BANANAS: Hello, Billy's girlfriend. God, Billy's girlfriends always make me feel so shabby!

BUNNY, *to Corrinna:* Arthur believes in keeping family skele-
  tons out in the open like pets. Heel, Bananas, heel!

LITTLE NUN, *running to Corrinna's side, to Corrinna:* I saw *The
  Sound of Music* thirty-one times. It changed my entire
  life.

CORRINNA: Unitarian.

ARTIE: All right now, where were we?

BUNNY: Ta Ta! The trumpet.

ARTIE, *at the piano, sings:*

> Back together again,
> Back together again . . .

HEAD NUN *screams:* There's Jackie Kennedy!!! Get me with
  Jackie Kennedy!!! *She puts her arm around the TV.*

The LITTLE NUN *takes out her Brownie with flash and takes a
picture of the head nun posing with Jackie on TV.*

SECOND NUN: There's Mayor Lindsay! Get me with him! Mayor Lindsay dreamboat! Mayor Wagner ugh!

There is a scream from the kitchen. BANANAS *has burned herself.*

ARTIE, *running into the kitchen:* What do you think you're doing?

BANANAS: Cooking for our guests. I'm some good, Artie. I can cook.

ARTIE: What is it?

BANANAS: Hamburgers. I felt for them and I cooked them.

ARTIE: Brillo pads. You want to feed our guests Brillo pads? *To the nuns:* Sisters, please, you're going to have to go into the other room. You're upsetting my wife. *He unplugs the TV and hustles the nuns off into Ronnie's bedroom.*

SECOND NUN: Go on with what you're doing. Don't bother about us. We're nothing. We've just given our lives up praying for you. I'm going to start picking who I pray for. *She exits.*

The LITTLE NUN *crosses to the kitchen to retrieve the peanut butter.*

BUNNY: That man is a saint. That woman is a devil.

BANANAS: I'm burned.

BUNNY: Put some vinegar on it. Some salt. Take the sting out.

HEAD NUN, *coming out of the bedroom, very pleased:* There is an altar boy in here. *She exits.*

BANANAS: My son was an altar boy. He kept us in good with God. But then he grew up. He isn't an altar boy any more. *She exits into her room.*

BUNNY, *to Corrinna:* Sometimes I think the whole world has
    gone cuckoo, don't you?
CORRINNA: For two days.

The LITTLE NUN *goes into Ronnie's room as* ARTIE *comes out
and downstage.*

ARTIE, *to us:* My son Ronnie's in there! He's been picked to be
    the Pope's altar boy at Yankee Stadium—out of all the
    boys at Fort Dix! I tell you—miracles tumble down on
    this family. I don't want you to meet him yet. If his
    mother sees him, her head will go all over the wall like
    Spanish omelettes.
    To Corrinna: Are you comfortable?
BUNNY: She's adorable! And so down to earth! *She takes Cor-
    rinna's bejeweled hands.*
CORRINNA: It's five carats. It's something, isn't it?
BUNNY, *to Corrinna:* Sit right up here with Mister Maestro—
    She seats Corrinna next to Artie at the piano.
ARTIE: Where was I—
BUNNY: "Like Fido chewed them." You left off there—
ARTIE *sings as* BUNNY *dances.* BANANAS *enters and watches them.*

> . . . Like Fido chewed them,
> But we're
> Back together again.
> You can say you knew us when
> We were together;
> Now we're apart,
> Thunder and lightning's
> Back in my heart,
> And that's the weather to be
> When you're back together with me.

BUNNY *claps wildly.* CORRINNA *follows suit.* BANANAS *claps slowly.*

BUNNY: Encore! Encore!

ARTIE, *happy now:* What should I play next?

BUNNY: Oh God, how do you pick a branch from a whole Redwood Forest?

BANANAS, *licking her hand:* "I Love You So I Keep Dreaming."

BUNNY *picks up the phone, but doesn't dial:* Come and get her!

BANANAS: Play "I Love You So I Keep Dreaming."

ARTIE, *pleased:* You really remember that?

BANANAS: How could I forget it . . .

BUNNY: I'm not used to being Queen of the Outsiders. What song is this?

ARTIE: I almost forgot it. It must have been like Number One that I ever wrote. The one that showed me I should go on.

BUNNY: Well, let me hear it.

ARTIE: You really surprise me, Bananas. Sometimes I miss you so much . . .

BUNNY, *warning:* Arthur, I still haven't forgiven you for this morning.

ARTIE *sings:*

> I love you so I keep dreaming
> Of all the lovely times we shared . . .

BUNNY: Heaven. That is unadulterated heaven.

BANANAS, *interrupting:* Now play "White Christmas"?

BUNNY: Shocks for sure.

BANANAS, *banging the keys of the piano:* Play "White Christmas"?

ARTIE, *to Corrinna:* She's . . . not feeling too . . . hot . . .

BUNNY, *to Corrinna:* In case you haven't noticed . . .

ARTIE: She keeps crawling under the weather . . . *He plays a run on the piano.*

BANANAS: "White Christmas"???????

ARTIE *groans, then plays and sings "White Christmas."*

BUNNY, *to Corrinna:* It really burns me up all these years The Telephone Hour doing salutes to fakers like Richard Rodgers. Just listen to that. Blaaaagh.

ARTIE *stops playing.*

BANANAS: Don't you hear it?

ARTIE *plays and sings slowly:*

> I'm dreaming of a . . .
> I love you so I . . .

They are the same tune.

ARTIE: Oh God. Oh God.

BANANAS *sings desperately:*

> I love you so I keep dreaming—

Are you tone deaf? Can't you hear it? *She bangs the keys on the piano.*

ARTIE *slams the lid shut on her hand. She yells and licks her fingers to get the pain off them.*

ARTIE: Oh, you have had it, Little Missy. All these years you knew that and made me play it. She's always trying to do that, Corrinna. Always trying to embarrass me. You have had it, Little Missy. Did Shakespeare ever write one original plot? You tell me that?

He drags Bananas down to the edge of the stage.

To us: In front of all of you, I am sorry. But you are looking at someone who has had it.

BANANAS: I am just saying your song sounds an awful lot like "White—

ARTIE: Then they can sing my song in the summertime. *He pushes her away and picks up the phone.*

BANANAS: Who are you calling?

BUNNY: Do it, Arthur.

BANANAS, *terrified:* Artie, who are you calling??????

BUNNY: Do you have a little suitcase? I'll start you packing.

BANANAS, *to Corrinna:* Billy's friend? Help me? Billy wouldn't want them to do this. Not to me. He'd be mad. *Whispering desperately, grabbing Corrinna's hands:* Help me? Bluebirds. He'll tell you all about it. Me walking on the roof. Can't you say anything? You want bribes? Here— take these flowers. They're for you. Take this liquor. For you. *She is hysterical.*

BUNNY *pulls her away and slaps her.*

BANANAS: I'll be quiet. I'll take my pills. *She reaches for the vial containing Corrinna's transistors and swallows them.*

CORRINNA, *to us:* My transistors!

ARTIE, *on the telephone:* This is Mr. Shaughnessy. Arthur M. . . . I was out there last week and talked about my wife.

BANANAS: That's why my ears were burning . . .

ARTIE: I forgot which doctor I talked to.

BANANAS: He had a mustache.

ARTIE: He had a mustache. *To his wife:* Thank you. *Into the phone:* Doctor? Hello? That's right, Doctor, could you come and . . . all that we talked about. The room over the garage is fine. Yes, Doctor. Now. Today. . . . Really? That soon? She'll be all ready. . . . *He hangs up the phone.*

BUNNY: Arthur, give me your hand. Like I said, today's my wedding day. I wanted something white at my throat. Look, downstairs in a pink cookie jar, I got a thousand dollars saved up and we are flying out to California with Corrinna. As soon as Bananas here is carted off, we'll step off that plane and Billy and you and I and Corrinna here will eat and dance and drink and love until the middle of the next full moon. *To Bananas:* Bananas, honey, it's not just a hospital. They got dances. *To Corrinna:* Corrinna, I'll be right back with my suitcase. *To Artie:* Artie, start packing. All my life I been treated like an old shoe. You turned me into a glass slipper. *She sings:*

I'm here with bells on.
Ring! Ring! Ring! Ring! Ring!

She exits.
ARTIE: I'm sorry. I'm sorry.

BANANAS *runs into her bedroom.*
CORRINNA *edges toward the front door.*

ARTIE: Well, Corrinna, now you know everything. Dirty laundry out in the open. I'll be different out West. I'm great at a party. I never took a plane trip before. I guess that's why my stomach is all queasied up. . . . Hey, I'd better start packing. . . . *He exits.*

CORRINNA *heads for the door. The* NUNS *enter.*

HEAD NUN: Miss Stroller! Miss Stroller! He told us all about Hollywood and Billy and Huckleberry Finn—

SECOND NUN: You tell Billy he ought to be ashamed treating a boy like that—

LITTLE NUN, *with paper and pen:* Miss Stroller, may I have your autograph?

CORRINNA: Sisters, pray for me? Pray my ears come out all right. I'm leaving for Australia—

THE NUNS: Australia?!?

CORRINNA: For a very major ear operation and I need all the prayers I can get. *To us:* South Africa's where they do the heart work, but Australia's the place for ears. So pray for me. Pray my operation's a success.

ARTIE *enters with his suitcase half-packed.*

ARTIE: Australia?

CORRINNA: I'm so glad I made a new friend my last day in America.

THE NUNS: She's going to Australia!

CORRINNA: Perhaps you'll bring me luck.

ARTIE: Your last day in America? Sisters, please.

CORRINNA: I'll be Mrs. Einhorn the next time you see me. . . . Billy and I are off to Australia tomorrow for two fabulous years. Billy's making a new film that is an absolute breakthrough for him—*Kangaroo*—and you must—all of you—come to California.

THE NUNS: *Kangaroo!* California!

CORRINNA: And we'll be back in two years.

ARTIE: But we're coming with you today . . .

The NUNS *are praying for Corrinna.*

LITTLE NUN: Our Father, Who art in heaven . . .

SECOND NUN: You shut up. I want to pray for her. Our Father—

HEAD NUN *blows a whistle:* I'll pray for her. *She sings:*

Ave Maria—

The THREE NUNS *sing "Ave Maria."*
RONNIE *enters wearing his army overcoat over the altar
boy's cassock and carrying the box with the bomb. He speaks
over the singing.*

RONNIE: Pop! Pop! I'm going!

ARTIE: Ronnie! Corrinna, this is the boy. *To us:* He's been
down to Fort Dix studying to be a general—

RONNIE: Pop, I'm going to blow up the Pope.

ARTIE: See how nice you look with your hair all cut—

The NUNS *have finished singing "Ave Maria" and take flash
pictures of themselves posing with Corrinna.*

RONNIE: Pop, I'm going to blow up the Pope and when *Time*
interviews me tonight, I won't even mention you. I'll say I
was an orphan.

ARTIE: Ronnie, why didn't you write and let me know you
were coming home? I might've been in California— It's
great to see you—

CORRINNA *runs to the front door, then stops:* Oh, wait a minute. The Pope's Mass at Yankee Stadium! I have two
tickets for the Pope's Mass at Yankee Stadium. Would
anybody like them?

The NUNS *and* RONNIE *rush Corrinna for the tickets, forcing
her back against the door.* RONNIE *wins the tickets and comes*

downstage to retrieve his gift-wrapped bomb. When he turns around to leave, the THREE NUNS *are advancing threateningly on him. They will not let him pass. They lunge at him. He runs into the bedroom for protection.*

ARTIE, *at the front door:* Miss Stroller, two years? Let's get this Australia part straight. Two years?

An M.P. *steps between Artie and Corrinna and marches into the room. The* M.P. *searches the room.*

ARTIE: Who are you? What are you doing here? Can I help you?

CORRINNA: Oh! This must be Ronnie! The son in the Army! I can't *wait* to hear all about you! *She embraces the* M.P.

The M.P. *hears the noises and fighting from Ronnie's room and runs in there.*

CORRINNA, *to Artie:* He looks just like you!

ARTIE, *following the* M.P.: You can't barge into a house like this—where are you going?

The LITTLE NUN *runs out of the bedroom, triumphantly waving the tickets, almost knocking Artie over.*

LITTLE NUN: I got 'em! I got 'em!

RONNIE *runs out after her. The other* TWO NUNS *run after him. The* M.P. *runs after them.* RONNIE *runs into the kitchen after the* LITTLE NUN, *who leaps over the couch.* RONNIE *leaps after her. He lands on top of her. He grabs the tickets.*

HEAD NUN, *to the* M.P.: Make him give us back our tickets.

M.P. *takes a deep breath and then:* Ronald-V.-Shaughnessy.-
You-are-under-arrest-for-being-absent-without-leave.-You-
have-the-right-to-remain-silent.-I-must-warn-you-that-any-
thing-you-say-may-be-used-against-you-in-a-military-court-
of-law.-You-have-the-right-to-counsel.-Do-you-wish-to-
call-counsel?

RONNIE *attempts escape. The* HEAD NUN *bears down on him.*

HEAD NUN: That altar boy stole our tickets!

SECOND NUN: Make him give them back to us!

RONNIE *throws the tickets down. The* HEAD NUN *grabs them.*

HEAD NUN, *to the little nun:* You! Back to Ridgewood! Yahoo!
She exits.

SECOND NUN, *to Corrinna:* Good luck with your ear operation.
She exits.

CORRINNA: This is an invitation—come to California.

RONNIE, *tossing the bomb to Corrinna:* From me to Billy—

CORRINNA: Oh, how sweet. I can't wait to open it. Hold the
elevator!! *She runs out.*

ARTIE, *to the* M.P., *who is struggling with Ronnie:* Hey, what
are you doing to my boy?!?

A MAN *dressed in medical whites enters.*

WHITE MAN: I got a radio message to pick up a Mrs. Arthur
M. Shaughnessy.

ARTIE: Bananas! *He runs to her bedroom.*

BUNNY, *dancing in through the front door, beaming and*

dressed like a million bucks: Ta Ta! Announcing Mrs.
Arthur M. Shaughnessy!

WHITE MAN: That's the name. Come along.

BUNNY, *to us, sings:*

> I'm here with bells on,
> Ringing out how I feel . . .

The WHITE MAN *slips the strait jacket on Bunny. She struggles.*
He drags her out. She's fighting wildly. ARTIE *returns.*

ARTIE: Wait. Stop.

RONNIE *pulls him from the door as there is a terrible explosion.*
Pictures fly off the wall. Smoke pours in from the hall.

BUNNY, *entering through the smoke:* Artie? Where's Corrinna? Where's Corrinna?

ARTIE: Corrinna?

ARTIE *runs out into the hall with* BUNNY.
The lights dim as RONNIE *and the* M.P. *grapple in slow motion,*
the LITTLE NUN *trying to pull the* M.P. *off Ronnie.*
BANANAS *comes downstage into the light. An unattached*
vacuum hose is wrapped around her shoulders. She cleans the
floor with the metallic end of the hose. She smiles at us.

BANANAS, *to us:* My house is a mess. . . . Let me straighten up.
. . . I can do that. . . . I'm a housewife. . . . I'm good for
something. . . . *She sings as she vacuums:*

> I love you so I keep dream . . .

She closes her eyes. Artie, you could salvage that song. You really could.

CURTAIN

SCENE 2

In the darkness after the curtain we hear the POPE *from Yankee Stadium. He gives his speech in heavily accented English. An announcer provides simultaneous translation in unaccented English.*

VOICE OF THE POPE: We feel, too, that the entire American people is here present with its noblest and most characteristic traits: a people basing its conception of life on spiritual values, on a religious sense, on freedom, on loyalty, on work, on the respect of duty, on family affection, on generosity and courage—

The curtain goes up.

It is later that night, and the only illumination in the room is the light from the television.

The house is vaguely picked up but not repaired, and everything is askew: neat—things are picked up off the floor, for instance—but lampshades are just tilted enough, pictures on the wall just slanted enough, and we see that everything that had been on the floor—the clothes, the suitcases—has been jammed into corners.

ARTIE *is watching the television.*

Another person is sitting in the easy chair in front of the TV.

—safeguarding the American spirit from those dangers which prosperity itself can entail and which the materialism of our day can make even more menacing. . . . From its brief but heroic history, this young and flourishing country can derive lofty and convincing examples to encourage us all in its future progress.

From the easy chair, we hear sobbing. The deep sobbing of a man.
ARTIE *clicks off the television and clicks on the lights. He has put a coat and tie over his green park clothes. He's very uncomfortable and is trying to be very cheery. The* MAN *in the chair keeps sobbing.*

ARTIE: I'm glad he said that. That Pope up at Yankee Stadium —some guy. Boy, isn't that Pope some guy. You ever met him in your travels? . . . You watch. That gang war in Vietnam—over tomorrow . . .
Brightly: People always talking about a certain part of the anatomy of a turkey like every Thanksgiving you say give me the Pope's nose. But that Pope is a handsome guy. Not as good-looking as you and me, but clean. Businesslike.
To us: This is the one. The only. You guessed it: this is Billy. He got here just before the eleven o'clock news. He had to identify Corrinna's body, so he's a little upset. You forgive him, okay?
Billy, come on—don't take it so hard. . . . You want to take off your shoes? . . . You want to get comfortable? . . . You want a beer? . . . *He sits at the piano and plays and sings:*

> If there's a broken heart
> For every light on Broadway,
> Screw in another bulb . . .

You like that? . . . Look, Billy, I'm sorry as hell we had to get together this way. . . . Look at it this way. It was quick. No pain. Pain is awful, but she was one of the luckies, Bill. She just went. And the apartment is all insured. They'll give us a new elevator and everything.

BILLY: The one thing she wanted was . . .

ARTIE: Come on, boy. Together. Cry, cry, get it all out.

BILLY: She wanted her footprints in Grauman's Chinese. I'm going to have her shoes set in wet cement. A ceremony. A tribute. God knows she'd hate it.

ARTIE: Hate it?

BILLY: Ahh, ever since the ears went, she stopped having the push, like she couldn't hear her different drummer any more, drumming up all that push to get her to the top. She just stopped. *He cries. Deep sobs.*

ARTIE, *uncomfortable:* She could've been one of the big ones. A lady Biggie. Boy. Stardust. Handfuls of it. All over her. Come on, boy . . . easy . . . easy . . . *Impatient:* Bill, that's enough.

BILLY: Do you have any tea bags?

ARTIE: You want a drink? Got the bourbon here—the Jack Daniels—

BILLY: No. Tea bags. Two. One for each eye.

ARTIE, *puzzled:* Coming right up. . . . *He goes into the kitchen and opens the cabinets.*

BILLY: Could you wet them? My future is all ashes, Artie. In the morning, I'll fly back with Corrinna's body, fly back to L.A. and stay there. I can't work. Not for a long, long time, if ever again. I was supposed to go to Australia, but no . . . all ashes. . . . *He puts one wet tea bag over each eye.* God, it's good to see you again, Artie.

ARTIE: Billy, you can't! You owe it—golly, Billy, the world— Bunny and me—we fell out of our loge seats—I'd be crazy if it wasn't for the laughs, for the romance you bring. You can't let this death stand in the way. Look what's happened to your old buddy. I've become this Dreaming Boy. I make all these Fatimas out of the future. Lourdes and Fatima. All these shrines out of the future and I keep crawling to them. Don't let that happen to you. Health. Health. You should make a musical. Listen to this. *He goes to the piano and plays and sings:*

> Back together again,
> Back together again . . .

BANANAS *appears in the bedroom doorway dressed in clothes that must have been very stylish and elegant ten years earlier.*

BILLY *starts:* Georgina!!

ARTIE *stops playing.*

BANANAS: No, Billy . . .
BILLY *stands up:* Oh God—for a minute I thought it was . . .
ARTIE: Don't she look terrific . . .
BILLY: Let me look at you. Turn around. *She does.* Jesus, didn't Georgina have good taste.
BANANAS, *turning:* I used to read *Vogue* on the newsstands to see what I'd be wearing in three years.
BILLY: Georgina took that dress right off her back and gave it to you. What a woman *she* was . . .

BILLY *is crying again.*

BANANAS: I put it on to make you happy, Billy.
ARTIE: Easy, Billy, easy . . .
BANANAS: It's a shame it's 1965. I'm like the best-dressed woman of 1954.
BILLY, *starting to laugh and cheer up:* You got the best of them all, Artie. Hello, Bananas!
BANANAS: Sometimes I curse you for giving me that name, Billy.
BILLY: A little Italian girl. What else was I going to call her?

The LITTLE NUN *rushes in from the bedroom, her habit wet.*

LITTLE NUN: Mr. Shaughnessy! Quick—the bathtub—the shower—the hot water is steaming—running over—I can't turn it—there's nothing to turn—

ARTIE *runs into the bedroom. The* LITTLE NUN *looks at Billy.*
BILLY *smiles at her. The* LITTLE NUN *runs into the bedroom.*
BANANAS *show him a spigot.*

BANANAS: I did it to burn her.
BILLY: Burn who?
BANANAS: Burn her downstairs. Have the hot water run through the ceiling and give her blisters. He won't like her so much when she's covered with blisters. Hot water can do that. It's one of the nicest properties of hot water.
BILLY: Burn who???
BANANAS: Kate Smith!! *She holds the spigot behind her back.*
ARTIE, *running in from the bedroom to the kitchen:* Wrench. Wrench. Screwdriver. *He rattles through drawers. Brightly, to Billy:* God, don't seem possible. Twenty years

ago. All started right on this block. Didn't we have some times? The Rainbow Room. Leon and Eddie's. I got the pictures right here.

The pictures are framed on the wall by the front door. BILLY *comes up to them.*

BILLY: Leon and Eddie's!
ARTIE, *indicating another picture:* The Village Barn.
BANANAS: The Village Barn. God, I loved the Village Barn.
ARTIE: It's closed, Bananas. Finished. Like you.
LITTLE NUN: Mr. Shaughnessy—please?

ARTIE *runs into the bedroom.*

LITTLE NUN: Mr. Einhorn?
BILLY: Hello?
LITTLE NUN: I was an usher before I went in and your name always meant quality. *She runs into the bedroom.*
BILLY: Why— Thank you ...
BANANAS: Help me, Billy? They're coming again to make me leave. Let me stay here? They'll listen to you. You see, they give me pills so I won't feel anything. Now I don't mind not feeling anything so long as I can remember feeling. You see? And this apartment, you see, here, right here, I stand in this corner and I remember laughing so hard. Doubled up. At something Ronnie did. Artie said. And I stand over here where I used to iron. When I could iron, I'd iron right here, and even then, the buttons, say, on button-down shirts could make me sob, cry ... and that window, I'd stand right here and mix me a rye-and-ginger pick-me-up and watch the lights go on in the Empire State Building and feel so tender ... unprotected.

... I don't mind not feeling so long as I can be in a place I remember feeling. You get me? You get me? Don't look at me dead. I'm no Georgina. I'm no Corrinna. Help me? Help Ronnie?

BILLY: Ronnie's in jail.

BANANAS: I don't mind the bars. But he can't take them. He's not strong like his mom. Come closer to me? Don't let them hear. *She strokes his eyebrows.* Oh, you kept your mustache. Nothing's changed. *She sings:*

Should auld acquaintance be forgot ...

ARTIE *comes out of the bedroom, soaking wet:* Those are eyebrows, Bananas. Eyebrows. Come on, where is it? *He reaches behind Bananas's back and pulls the silver faucet handle from her clenched fist.* Billy, you see the wall I'm climbing? *He goes back into the bedroom with it.*

The LITTLE NUN *looks out into the living room.*

LITTLE NUN, *to Billy:* We never got introduced.

BILLY: Do I know you?

BANANAS *goes into the corner by the window.*

LITTLE NUN, *coming into the room:* No, but my two friends died with your friend today.

BILLY: I'm very sorry for you.

LITTLE NUN: No, it's all right. All they ever wanted to do was die and go to heaven and meet Jesus. The convent was very depressing. Pray a while. Scream a while. Well, they got their wish, so I'm happy.

BILLY: If your friends died with my friend, then that makes

us—oh God! Bananas! That makes us all friends! You
friends and me friends and we're all friends!

BANANAS: Help Ronnie. Help him. *She hands Billy the phone.*

BILLY, *on the phone:* Operator—my friend the operator—get
me person-to-person my friend General Buckley Revere
in the Pentagon—202 LIncoln 5-5600.

ARTIE, *coming out of the bedroom:* No, Billy . . . no favors for
Ronnie. The kid went AWOL. M.P.'s dragging him out
of the house. You think I like that? *To Bananas:* That
kid's your kid, Bananas. You got the crazy monopoly on
all the screwball chromosomes in that kid.

BILLY: Buck? Bill.

ARTIE, *to Bananas:* Let him learn responsibility. Let him learn
to be a man.

BILLY: Buck, just one favor: my godchild, Ron Shaughnessy.
He's in the brig at Fort Dix. He wanted to see the Pope.

ARTIE, *to Bananas:* Billy and me served our country. You think
Billy could call up generals like that if he wasn't a veteran!
To us: I feel I got to apologize for the kid. . . . I tried to
give him good strong things . . .

BILLY: Buck, has the Army lost such heart that it won't let a
simple soldier get a glimpse of His Holiness . . .

The front door opens. BUNNY *enters. She looks swell and great
and all the Webster Dictionary synonyms for terrific. She's all
exclamation points: pink and white!!! She carries an open umbrella and a steaming casserole in her potholder-covered
hands.*

BUNNY: Arthur, are you aware *The Rains of Ranchipur* are
currently appearing on my ceiling?

ARTIE: Ssshhhhhhh. . . . *Indicating her pot:* Is that the veal and
oranges?

BUNNY: That's right, Arthur. I'm downstairs making veal and oranges and what do I get from you? Boiling drips.

ARTIE: That's Billy. . . . Billy's here. *He takes the umbrella from her.*

BUNNY: Billy Einhorn here? And you didn't call me? Oh, Mr. Einhorn. *She steps into the room. She is beaming. She poses.* And that's why the word Voilà was invented. Excuse my rudeness. Hi, Artie. Hi, Bananas.

BILLY, *on the phone:* Thank you, Buck. Yes, Yes, Terrific, Great. Talk to you tomorrow. Love ya. Thank you. *He hangs up.* Ronnie'll be all right. Buck will have him stationed in Rome with NATO. He'll do two weeks in the brig just to clear the records. . . .

ARTIE: Then off to Rome? Won't that be interesting. And educational. Thank you, Billy. Thank you.

BILLY: Ronnie's lucky. Buck said everybody at Dix is skedded for Vietnam.

BUNNY: I wouldn't mind that. I love Chinese food.

ARTIE: That's the little girl from the steambath . . .

BILLY *notices Bunny. They laugh.*

BUNNY: Hi! I'm Bunny from right down below.

BILLY *kisses her hand.*

BUNNY: Oohhhh. . . . Artie, perhaps our grief-stricken visitor from Movieland would join us in a Snack à la Petite.

BILLY: No, no.

ARTIE: Come on, Bill.

BUNNY: Flying in on such short notice you must have all the starving people of Armenia in your tumtum, begging, "Feed me, feed me."

BILLY: Just a bite would be—

BANANAS *comes down to us with Artie's scrapbook:* What they
do is they make a scrapbook of all the things she can cook,
then they paste them in the book—veal parmagina, eggplant meringue...

ARTIE *grabs it from her.*

BANANAS: Eughh...

ARTIE, *to Billy:* We make a scrapbook of all the things Bunny
can cook, you see, then we paste them in the book.

BUNNY *serves.* ARTIE *takes a deep breath. He tastes.*

ARTIE, *to us:* I wish I had spoons enough for all of you.

They eat.

BUNNY: Mr. Einhorn, I met your friend today before Hiro-
shima Mon Amour happened out there and all I got to
say is I hope when I go I got two Sisters of Charity with
me. I don't know your persuasion God-wise, but your
friend Corrinna, whether she likes it or not, is right up
there in heaven tonight.

BILLY: Artie, you were right. We are what our women make
us. Corrinna: how easily deaf becomes dead. It was her
sickness that held us together. Health. Health. You were
always healthy. You married a wonderful little Italian
girl. You have a son. Where am I?

BUNNY: Deaf starlets. That's no life.

BILLY: So how come she's dead? Who blew her up?

BANANAS: It was on the eleven o'clock news.

BUNNY: Crying and explanations won't bring her back. Mr.

Einhorn, if it took all this to get you here, I kiss the
calendar for today. Grief puts erasers in my ears. My
world is kept a beautiful place. Artie . . . I feel a song
coming on.

ARTIE: How about a lovely tune, Bill, to go with that food. *He
goes to the piano and plays.*

BUNNY *opens the umbrella and does a dance with it, as she
sings:*

>Where is the devil in Evelyn?
>What's it doing in Angela's eyes?
>Evelyn is heavenly,
>Angela's in a devil's disguise.
>I know about the sin in Cynthia
>And the hell in Helen of Troy,
>But where is the devil in Evelyn?
>What's it doing in Angela's eyes?
>Oh boy!
>What's it doing in Angela's eyes?

BILLY: My God!

ARTIE, *up from the piano:* What!

BILLY: Suddenly!

BANANAS: Was it the veal?

BILLY: I see future tenses! I see I can go on! Health! I have an
extra ticket. Corrinna's ticket. For Australia.

ARTIE: God, Billy, I'd love to. I have all my music . . . ARTIE
races to Billy.

BILLY, *coming to Bunny:* Cook for me a while? Stay with me
a while? In two hours a plane leaves from Kennedy and
on to a whole new world. Los Angeles. We drop off
Corrinna's body. Then on to Hawaii. Samoa. Nonstop to
Melbourne. Someone who listens. That's what I need.

BUNNY: But my whole life is here ...

BILLY: Chekhov was right. Work. Work. That's the only answer. All aboard ? ? ? ? ? ?

BUNNY: My my my my my my my ...

ARTIE: Are you out of your head? Leaving in two hours? It takes about six months to get shots and passports—

BUNNY: Luckily two years ago I got shots and a passport in case I got lucky with a raffle ticket to Paree. *To us:* I'm in raffles all over the place.

ARTIE: Bunny—

BUNNY: Leave me alone, Arthur. I have to think. I don't know what to say. It's all so sudden.

The LITTLE NUN *comes out of the bedroom. She is in civvies. As a matter of fact, she has on one of Georgina's dresses, off the shoulder, all covered with artificial cherries. It is too big for her. She carries her wet habit.*

LITTLE NUN: I was catching a cold so I put on one of your dresses, Mrs. Shaughnessy. I have to go now. I want to thank you for the loveliest day I've ever had. You people are so lucky. You have so much. *She is near tears.* And your son is so cute. Maybe when I take my final vows I can cross my fingers and they won't count.

BILLY: How would you like to stay here?

ARTIE: Stay here?

BILLY: There'll be an empty apartment right down below and you could come up and take care of Bananas. *He takes out his wallet and gives a number of hundred-dollar bills to the little nun.* How's this for a few months' salary?

ARTIE: What's all that money?

BILLY: Artie, don't send Bananas away. Love. That's all she needs.

BANANAS: It is? *The telephone rings. She answers it:* Yes? Yes?
*To Artie, who is on his knees, trying to reason with
Bunny:* It's the Zoo.

ARTIE: Tell them I'll call—what are they calling this late for?

BANANAS: The animals are all giving birth! Everything's having a baby. The leopards and the raccoons and the gorillas
and the panthers and the ...

ARTIE, *taking the phone:* Who is this? Al? Look, this is what
you have to do. Heat the water. Lock the male elephants
out. They get testy. The leopardess tends to eat her children. Watch her careful ...

As he talks on the phone so we can't hear him, BUNNY *comes
downstage and talks to us.*

BUNNY: The Pope saw my wish today. He looked me right in
the eye and he winked. Hey! Smell—the bread is starting
again and there's miracles in the air! The Pope is flying
back through the nighttime sky and all the planets fall
back into place and Orion the Hunter relaxes his bow ...
and the gang war in Vietnam will be over and all those
crippled people can now stand up and walk back to
Toledo. And, Billy, in front of all these people, I vow to
you I'll be the best housekeeper money can buy ... and
I'll cook for you and clean and, who knows, maybe
there'll be a development. ... And, Bananas, honey, when
I get to California, I'll send you some of my clothes. I'll
keep up Georgina's traditions. Sister, here are the keys to
my apartment downstairs. You can write a book, "I Jump
Over the Wall," and, Billy, you could film it.

ARTIE, *on the phone:* Yes! I'll be right down. I'll be right on
the subway. Yes. *He hangs up.* I ... have to go to work.

... Billy? Bun? Would you like to come? See life starting? It's beautiful.

BUNNY, *in the kitchen:* Bananas, honey, could I have this cop-
per pot? I've always had my eye on this pot.

BANANAS: Take it.

ARTIE: Listen, Bill.

BUNNY: Well, I'm packed.

ARTIE: I write songs, Bill. *He starts playing and singing "Back
Together Again."*

BANANAS, *to Billy, who is on his way out:* Thank you, Billy.

BILLY*, coming back and sitting alongside Artie:* Artie, can I
tell you a secret?

ARTIE *stops playing.*

BILLY: Do you know who I make my pictures for? Money?
No. Prestige? No. I make them for you.

ARTIE: Me?

BILLY: I sit on the set and before every scene I say, "Would
this make Artie laugh? Would this make Artie cry?"

ARTIE: I could come on the set and tell you personal ...

BILLY: Oh no, Artie. If I ever thought you and Bananas weren't
here in Sunnyside, seeing my work, loving my work, I
could never work again. You're my touch with reality.
He goes to Bananas. Bananas, do you know what the
greatest talent in the world is? To be an audience. Anybody can create. But to be an audience ... be an audience ...

ARTIE *runs back to the piano. He sings desperately:*

I'm looking for something,
I've searched everywhere ...

BUNNY: Artie, I mean this in the best possible sense: You've
   been a wonderful neighbor.
BILLY, *to Artie:* I just saved your life.

BILLY *takes Bunny's hand and leads her out.*
ARTIE *plays "Where Is the Devil in Evelyn?" hysterically, then
runs out after them, carrying his sheet music.*

ARTIE, *shouting:* Bill! Bill! I'm too old to be a young talent!!!

The LITTLE NUN *comes downstage, her hands filled with
money.*

LITTLE NUN, *to us:* Life is this orchard and we walk beneath it
   and apples and grapes and cherries and mangoes all tum-
   ble down on us. Ask and you shall receive. I didn't even
   ask and look how much I have. Thank you. Thank you
   all.
   She kisses the television. A shrine . . . I wanted to be a
   Bride of Christ but I guess now I'm a young divorcee.
   I'll go downstairs and call up the convent. Good-bye.
   Thank you. *She wrings out her wet habit, then throws it
   up in the air and runs out.*

BANANAS *turns off all the lights in the room.* ARTIE *returns.
He stands in the doorway.* BANANAS *sits on the edge of the
armchair. She is serene and peaceful and beautiful in the dim
light.* ARTIE *comes into the room slowly. He lets his music
slip to the floor.*

BANANAS: I don't blame you for that lady, Artie. I really don't.
   But I'm going to be good to you now. Cooking. I didn't
   know you liked cooking. All these years and I didn't

know you liked cooking. See, you can live with a person . . . Oh God, Artie, it's like we're finally alone for the
first time in our life. Like it's taken us eighteen years to
get from the church to the hotel room and we're finally
alone. I promise you I'll be different. I promise you . . .

He smiles at her, hopefully.

Hello, Artie.

*She sits on her haunches like a little dog smiling for food.
She sings:*

> Back together again,
> Back together again.
> Since we split up
> The skies we lit up
> Looked all bit up
> Like Fido chewed them,
> But they're
> Back together again.
> You can say you knew us when . . .

*She barks. She sits up, begging, her hands tucked under her
chin. She rubs her face into Artie's legs. He pats her head.
She is thrilled. He kneels down in front of her. He touches
her face. She beams. She licks his hand. He kisses her. He
strokes her throat. He looks away. He holds her. He kisses
her fully. She kisses him. He leans into her. As his hands
go softly on her throat, she looks up at him with a beautiful
smile as if she had always been waiting for this. He kisses
her temples, her cheeks. His hands tighten around her throat.
Their bodies blend as he moves on top of her. She smiles
radiantly at him. He squeezes the breath out of her throat.
She falls.*

   Soft piano music plays.

The stage begins to change. Blue leaves begin to filter all over the room until it looks like ARTIE *is standing in a forest of leaves that are blue. A blue spotlight appears downstage and he steps into it. He is very happy and smiles at us.*

ARTIE: Hello. My name is Artie Shaughnessy and I'd like to thank you for that blue spot and to sing you some songs from the pen of. *He sings:*

> I'm here with bells on,
> Ringing out how I feel.
> I'll ring,
> I'll roar,
> I'll sing
> Encore!
> I'm here with bells on.
> Ring! Ring! Ring!

The stage is filled with blue leaves.

CURTAIN

LANDSCAPE
OF THE
BODY

THIS PLAY IS FOR
ADELE CHATFIELD-TAYLOR

CHARACTERS

Betty
Captain Marvin Holahan
Rosalie
Raulito
Bert
Donny
Joanne
Margie
Masked Man
Durwood Peach
Dope King of Providence
Bank Teller

On a ferry to Nantucket and in
Greenwich Village.

MUSIC AND LYRICS FOR ALL SONGS BY JOHN GUARE

Landscape of the Body was first produced by William Gardner at the Academy Festival Theatre, in Lake Forest, Illinois, in July 1977. It was directed by John Pasquin.

CAST

BETTY	*Shirley Knight*
CAPTAIN MARVIN HOLAHAN	*F. Murray Abraham*
ROSALIE	*Peg Murray*
RAULITO	*Richard Bauer*
BERT	*Paul McCrane*
DONNY	*Anthony Marciona*
JOANNE	*Alexa Kenin*
MARGIE	*Bonnie Deroski*
MASKED MAN	*Jay Sanders*
DURWOOD PEACH	*Rex Robbins*
DOPE KING OF PROVIDENCE	*Jay Sanders*
BANK TELLER	*Jay Sanders*

The settings were by John Wulp. Costumes were by Laura Crow. The lighting was by Jennifer Tipton. The stage mechanics were by Robert Giffen. The production pianists were Rod Derefinko and William Snyder. The stage manager was Stephen McCorkle.

Landscape of the Body was then presented in New York City, by Joseph Papp at the Public Theatre (New York Shakespeare Festival) on October 12, 1977. It was directed by John Pasquin.

CAST

BETTY	*Shirley Knight*
CAPTAIN MARVIN HOLAHAN	*F. Murray Abraham*
ROSALIE	*Peg Murray*
RAULITO	*Richard Bauer*
BERT	*Paul McCrane*
DONNY	*Anthony Marciona*
JOANNE	*Alexa Kenin*
MARGIE	*Bonnie Deroski*
MASKED MAN	*Raymond J. Barry*
DURWOOD PEACH	*Remak Ramsay*
DOPE KING OF PROVIDENCE	*Raymond J. Barry*
BANK TELLER	*Raymond J. Barry*

The settings and costumes were by Santo Loquasto. Lighting was by Jennifer Tipton. Musical arrangements and incidental music were by Wally Harper. The associate producer was Bernard Gersten. The pianist was Rod Derefinko. The stage manager was Stephen McCorkle.

A C T   O N E

———

The deck of a ferry boat sailing from Hyannisport to Nantucket.

A woman sits writing notes on the deck. She is bundled up in layers of clothes against the cool. She has shopping bags around her feet. When she finishes one note, she rolls it into a cylinder and inserts it into a bottle she takes out of the shopping bags. She seals the bottle and tosses it overboard. She watches it go. She begins another.

A man is watching her. He is heavily disguised. Comic false eyeglasses and nose with mustache dangling beneath. Muffler wrapped high. Hat pulled down. He carries a little suitcase.

MAN: That's the Kennedy compound over there. I bought a
    postcard at the bus station in Hyannisport and the post-
    card tells you whose house is who. *He proffers it. She
    looks at it briefly, looks at the shore, and resumes her
    note writing.*

That house is Teddy Kennedy's and that house was where Jack lived and that house is where the parents lived and that house is where the sister Eunice lived and that house is where the sister Jean lived and that house—the postcard seems not to match up to reality. I get them all mixed up now, it's been so long. Empty rooms. Open windows. White curtains blowing out.

She looks up, tosses another bottle over, and watches it go.

I won a contest in grammar school knowing the names of the Dionne Quintuplets. I could rattle them off. Emilie. Annette. See. I can't even remember. Yvonne. And the worst is nobody remembers the Dionne Quintuplets. You tell young people, younger than we are, about the Dionne Quintuplets and they don't know who you're talking about.

WOMAN: Emilie was the left-handed one. Emilie was the only left-handed Dionne Quintuplet. What was the name of the doctor who delivered the Dionne Quintuplets?

MAN: Dr. Dafoe.

WOMAN: Dr. Dafoe.

MAN: We could have a marriage made in heaven sharing information like that.

WOMAN: I'm not in the market.

MAN: I went down to Washington in 1960 for Kennedy's inauguration. They were selling at the Union Station an entire set of dishes of china and every plate was a different Kennedy. The big meat platter was Poppa Joe. The other cake platter had Momma Rose on it. John-John and Caroline were on little bread-and-butter plates. You're so open to talk to. Generally on trips of this nature—two-hour ferry trips from the mainland to an island—you

begin talking to your fellow shipmates desperately leaping into conversational gambits, reduced to buying dusty
postcards of abandoned compounds of families who once
made all the difference in America. I begin talking and
you pick right up on it. We could have a marriage made
in heaven. We can talk. I think that's why marriages fail.
People can't talk. People fight to have something to talk
about. People kill each other, say, because the words won't
come into place. I think of murder, say, as a sentence that
did not make it through the computer up here in the head.
If people had a better grasp of language, of syntax, of the
right word, of being understood, you'd hear that crime
rate, you'd see that homicide rate plunge like those bottles
you're tossing over . . . would they be sentences you'd be
writing on that piece of paper?

She tosses another bottle over.

What attracted you to me first? My confidence-inspiring
voice? My ability to select the proper word out of the
autumn air? A poll said what women notice most in men
was their butts. Is that it? You liked my ass? Is that what
attracted you to me? Are the polls right? My confidence is
in bad disrepair and needs all the propping up it can beg,
borrow, or infer.

WOMAN: I saw you getting on the boat. I wondered if you were
in disguise. I said to myself, is this a masquerade cruise?
Then I thought, this is a man with a facial cancer and his
face has been removed and replaced by a necessary false
nose to disguise the two gaping holes under there. A false
mustache to cover the missing upper lip. False eyebrows
to cover the grafted skin around the eyeballs which still
function or he'd be tapping a white cane around this deck.

He walks with a steady stride. No, I won't have to be yelling Man Overboard. It's a disguise.

MAN: You recognized me?

WOMAN: Captain Marvin Holahan. Sixth Precinct Homicide.

The man pulls off his disguise.

HOLAHAN: What did you write in that note? A confession?

*She throws sheets of small papers into the wind. They blow
away. She pours bottles overboard.*

WOMAN: A confession. A full confession. I wrote down everything that happened. And it's all gone. There it goes!
There's your case.

*They face each other. The lights go down on them. They each
take off their coats. The light is harsh in this interrogation
room. She sits down in a chair. He circles her. He shines a desk
lamp in her eyes.*

VOICE: Flashback. Five months before. Marvin Holahan. Betty
Yearn. Sixth Precinct. New York City. A spring day.
Easter Sunday. Vernal equinoxes. The sun and moon cross
each other's path.

BETTY: I don't see how you can ask me these questions.

HOLAHAN: Easy.

BETTY: At this point in my life in history you could ask me
these questions.

HOLAHAN: The kid is dead.

BETTY: I cannot cannot cannot—draw underlines under the
cannot—cannot cannot cannot—six negatives make a positive—cannot understand—

HOLAHAN: How I can ask you these questions?

BETTY: How you can ask me these questions—

HOLAHAN: Lady, I'm not talking simple child-battering.

BETTY: The kid is dead. The kid is dead. You leave out the fact it's my kid.

HOLAHAN: Decapitation, Betty.

BETTY: My son is dead. My boy is dead. My kid killed. Not *the* kid. My kid.

HOLAHAN: The head chopped off, Betty. That's not Family Court. Chopped-off heads are not referrals to Family Counseling. That goes beyond child battering.

BETTY: Not *the* kid. *My* kid. *My* kid.

HOLAHAN: You and your boyfriend didn't say my kid when you got out the hacksaw. You must've said, oh, let me guess: you little bastard.

BETTY: I'm not going to throw up.

HOLAHAN: What did your kid see, Betty, that you had to chop his head off?

BETTY: If I throw up, it's like you win. You're not going to win.

HOLAHAN: Where's the boy's father?

BETTY: I haven't seen him in years.

HOLAHAN: Maybe the boy's father did it in revenge against you?

BETTY: Strangers don't do revenge. The father didn't even know where we live. I feel like I'm standing in that corner over there watching me, and if I try hard enough I can switch the dial and I'll see me on another channel. I'd like a laugh track around my life. I'd like a funny theme introducing my life. I'm standing right over there in that corner watching me.

HOLAHAN: Was your boy homosexual?

BETTY: He's fourteen, for God's sake.

HOLAHAN: Lady, we got bodies coming in here don't even live

to be fourteen. Their ages never get off the fingers of two hands.

BETTY: There's a whole series of homosexual murders going on down there at Christopher Street. Maybe the kid was into something. I don't think so. Don't those murders involve decap—the heads off . . .

HOLAHAN: How do you know about that?

BETTY: Is that the clue that gives myself away? I read the papers. I hear on the street. Did you follow up that clue? Why did you drag me in here? I'm supposed to be out there, mourning, weeping—

HOLAHAN: Betty, I'm trying to be kind. If you're embarrassed confessing to such a heinous crime, you want me to get Sergeant Lorraine Dean down here? There ain't nothing Lorraine hasn't heard. She's a good woman, a good listener, heavy in the ankles, platinum blonde, a nice soft bosom that I swear she keeps Seconal and Libriums in. She'd hold you and rock you in the cradle of the deep and she'll sing "I'm confessing that I love you . . ." She'll sing that and make it easy for you to talk about what you did and get you help. She's got a nice voice Lorraine does. She could've made it big in the show biz department were it not for her tragedy in the ankle department. Should I get Lorraine down here and you can tell her all? You want Lorraine? "I just found joy. I'm as happy as a baby boy. With another brand new choo choo toy when I marry my Lorraine!" Betty? You could tell me too? There's nothing hasn't been poured into these ears. I'm taking courses at NYU nights in psychology. Things like you did happen all the time. We even had a spot quiz last week on a woman, went into a deep depression, drowned her two kids. Two! You just did one. Imagine how she feels.

But they were infants. And she drowned them. I can't
wait to ask my teacher about decapitation. You might
help me get an honors. I might do a paper on you. Most
infanticides are drownings or smotherings or an occasional throwing off a bridge ...

BETTY: I remember when I was a little kid at the end of the
McCarthy hearings when Joe McCarthy was destroying
human lives, this great lawyer—

HOLAHAN: Welch. Joseph Welch.

BETTY: Stood up and said to McCarthy Is there no such thing
as human decency? And that question shocked everybody
and destroyed Joe McCarthy.

HOLAHAN: I'll tell you that great lawyer Welch after that made
a film for Otto Preminger called *Anatomy of a Murder*
starring James Stewart and Lee Remick. Is there no such
thing as human decency left?

BETTY: Is there no such thing as human decency left?

HOLAHAN: A damn good little question.

BETTY: Will I get off to go to my son's funeral?

HOLAHAN: Is Otto Preminger filming it?

BETTY: Am I booked? What's up? Do I go to my son's funeral?

HOLAHAN: Did you kill him?

BETTY: Do I get off for the funeral?

HOLAHAN: Say yes, beautiful Betty, and there's no place you
can't go.

BETTY: I want my boy buried in Bangor, Maine, with his
grandparents and his aunts and his uncles. I want him
buried in Bangor with my father, with my sister Rosalie.
Where I'll be buried when I die. I want him there. I want
him out of New York.

HOLAHAN: You think it's fair to be at the funeral when you
caused the funeral?

BETTY: I'm sorry, Your Honor, Mr. Kangaroo Court. I missed his death.

HOLAHAN: I keep thinking you were there.

BETTY: What is my motive? I cannot believe I am a suspect in my own son's death. I am supposed to be comforted. I am supposed to be held and allowed to cry and not made to feel . . . there's no insurance. I am no beneficiary. I cannot believe. I don't kill my own flesh and blood. I don't kill me. If I wanted to kill him, I would've killed me along with him. I don't kill me. I am here. Am I a car? A car you have to pull over to the side of the road and give a ticket to? You have to torture a certain number of people a day? Is this torture a routine formality? My boy is dead. I would like to grieve.

HOLAHAN: When did you come to New York?

BETTY: Two years ago.

HOLAHAN: Why?

BETTY: To get my sister.

HOLAHAN: Where is your sister now?

BETTY: My sister's dead.

HOLAHAN: Let me get this straight. You came to New York two years ago to get your dead sister.

BETTY: She was not dead at the time.

HOLAHAN: You came to New York two years ago alone to get your sister.

BETTY: Not alone. With Bert.

HOLAHAN: Bert? Bert?

BETTY: My kid.

HOLAHAN: The one you killed. Ah, yes, that Bert.

A redhead appears out of the dark. She's very tough, very blowsy. A good sport. Her name is Rosalie.

ROSALIE: They're getting you for your life style, kid. They can't stand it that you got the life style of the future and they're stuck here in their little precincts.

BETTY: I'm being prosecuted for my life style. You can't stand it that I got the life style of the future and you're stuck here in your little precinct.

ROSALIE *embraces Betty and comforts her. Rosalie goes back into the dark.*

HOLAHAN: Bert's body was found yesterday afternoon floating off an abandoned pier at the bottom of Charles Street in a particularly seedy part of Greenwich Village. The boy's head was found floating close by. No signs of sexual molestation. But the boy was not killed there. The murder took place someplace else. The body was taken and dumped off this abandoned pier notorious for sexual pick-ups between members shall we say of the same sex and for the exchange of narcotic goods exchanged between people so spaced out they don't know what sex they are. From the boy's school pass, we find where he lives on Christopher Street, a notorious street in the self-same Greenwich Village. We find evidence in the boy's apart-ment where he lives with his mother, we find evidences of blood in his own home. In the bathroom. The boy was murdered and decapitated in the bathroom of his own legal abode. The mother lived there with the boy. The mother is a hotsy-totsy we find out. The mother works in porno films.

BETTY: Soft core.

HOLAHAN: *Do Me Do Me Do Me Till It Falls Off* does not sound soft core to me. *Leather Sheets* does not sound soft core to me. Vaginal penetration recorded in medical detail by a sixteen-millimeter camera owned by Mafia people does not sound soft core to me.

BETTY: That wasn't me in all of them. My sister worked in porno films. I was finishing up a contract she had made shortly before her death.

HOLAHAN: And when you appear on *What's My Line?* How do you sign in, please?

BETTY: I work in a travel agency.

HOLAHAN: A fake travel agency.

RAULITO, *a Cuban in a trench coat, appears out of the dark.*

RAULITO: Honeymoon Holidays was not fake.

HOLAHAN: Closed down for selling fraudulent trips—

RAULITO: It don't harm nobody to start off a marriage with a good honeymoon.

RAULITO *goes back into the dark.* BETTY *takes pills out of her pocket.* HOLAHAN *knocks them out.*

HOLAHAN: No junkie shit here, baby.

BETTY: They're Tums for the tummy, asshole. I don't want to throw up. If I do not throw up, it will somehow prove to me that I am not on your level, that I possess a strength, am the proud possessor of a dignity—

HOLAHAN: And yet Miss Dignity seems to appear in these loops. We raided Dirty Mort's on Forty-Second Street. We ran the loops. I remembered your face from the loops when they brought you in. I had long said to myself what kind of person would allow another human being to urinate on her while a Mafia-run camera was whirring away. Little did I think, Miss Life Style of the Future, I would have the honor of having met you. As you see, I am a movie buff. Those films. These films. This doesn't look like anybody's sister to me. This looks coincidentally like you. Or maybe it's Gene Kelly in outtakes from *Singin' in the Rain*? What kind of human being allows herself to be treated in this way? I hate you, baby.

BETTY: No shit, Dick Tracy. I thought this was a love story.

HOLAHAN: When I was a kid my parents chained me to the piano so I'd play. I was a fat kid, too, so the chains had a double purpose. The pressure of them would stop me eating and force me to play. I eat, baby. I eat the right amounts and I am thin and I play the piano very well. And I also know all about family hatred. I know that families are there to learn your deepest secrets and betray you with their intimacy. Your kid must've found out too much about you. Your kid, I'm beginning to see, cramped your style. Of course! Every kid thinks his mother is the Virgin Mary, for Christ's sake, and one day your kid sees the films you work in when you're not in the fake travel agency. I get it! And I find it a fantastic fact that a woman who gives head in twenty-five-cent loops should be in here for taking head. To get rid of the son's head that contained the eyes that saw her life.

BETTY: Are you nuts?

HOLAHAN: Because his eyes turned into these Mason jars preserving the disgust at what you had become.

BETTY: I want out of here! *She bangs on doors.* That's not me in those films. That's my sister.

HOLAHAN: Oh sure. Your sister. Bring her in here. Testify for you.

BETTY: She's dead.

HOLAHAN: When?

BETTY: A year ago, last October.

RAULITO *appears.*

RAULITO: Is that what happened to you?

ROSALIE *appears.*

BETTY: She was walking on Hudson Street.
ROSALIE: I was just walking on Hudson Street.
BETTY: A cyclist hit her.
HOLAHAN: And Raulito?
BETTY: He's dead.

RAULITO *and* ROSALIE *go in the black.*

HOLAHAN: You're a terrific dame to know. All the people connected to you via the avenue of blood die in one year. Maybe I'll go to Bangor, Maine, and dig your sister up.
BETTY: I'm really grateful to you.
HOLAHAN: The Grateful Dead. The noted rock group.
BETTY: I am alive, detective. Because I am, I *was* going crazy from my kid's murder. When they came and told me the kid was dead, they could've fit me for a strait jacket at the same time they were fitting him for a shroud. You have actually taken my mind off it. My loathing for you replaces my grief. I mean, my fury is real. You're nuts.
HOLAHAN: Do you deny you made golden shower films where people urinated on you?
BETTY: That was my sister.
HOLAHAN: Oh, this is one of those movies where there's a good twin and an evil twin.
BETTY: You got movies on the brain. It must make life easy for you. You can just put anything you want into a movie and that explains everything.

HOLAHAN: One good twin. One bad twin. Was it the good twin
or the bad twin who made those animal films? *Barnyard
Bimbo. Six With a Pig.* An alleged human being has sex
with a German shepherd. Is that the sister? It looks a hell
of a lot like the good twin sitting right here in her little
Mary Janes and golden braids.

BETTY: I did it for the money.

HOLAHAN: Of all the motives, that still has to be my favorite
motive. I did it for the money.

BETTY: My sister was in the hands of the mob. She owed them
money. She was a junkie. They forced me to make the
films to work off the bread she owed them for smack.

HOLAHAN: After "I did it for the money" my next favorite
motive is the Mob made me do it. Get the Mob. The Mob
did this, the Mob did that. The Mob must be pretty busy.
That's some pretty busy Mob. My heart goes out to the
Mob more and more every day. Nothing better than
having a convenient fall guy. I'm sorry, Betty. I look to
the family. I go right to the scene of the crime between
those shapely gams. The family, Betty.

BETTY: You're a class act, Detective. Detective Marvin Holahan. *Detective That's Entertainment Parts One and Two
and Three and Four.* What are you? Some faggot out to
get me because—

HOLAHAN: I know everything about you.

BETTY: You don't know nothing about me except I posed for
some sleazy pictures and who cares. But I know about you.
They chained you to a piano so you wouldn't eat and you
would play. And you do both and you're a good boy. A
lot of things happened to me, but nobody ever chained
me to a piano and you know what? I didn't throw
up. I can look you right in the eye. I didn't throw up.
I won.

The interrogation room goes dark. Lights come up on Rosalie.
A piano swings into view. Music plays at the piano. ROSALIE
sings to us in the audience. She's really good-natured, has a
swell voice, moves like a stripper.

ROSALIE:

> Hey Stay a While
> In the crook of my arms
> All you got to do is
> Look in my arms
> And you'll see Home Sweet Home
> I'll invest in a doormat
> Hey Home Sweet Home
> We'll test the mattress
> Our arms are sinuous
> All performances are continuous
> Hey Stay a While
> Feel the smile in my arms
> And the smile's in my arms
> All for you
> Sit back/Relax
> Cool brow/Tension slacks
> Hey Stay a While
> My arms are filled with
> What the whole world lacks
> Hey Stay a While

Being dead is not the worst thing in the world. Is there
life after death? I dare ask the question: Is there life before death? The good thing about being dead is at least
you know where you stand. You have one piece of information in life and you think life means this. Then you

get a new piece of info and everything you knew means something else. The scary thing about death is how comfortable it is. Finally giving in to the drowning. Life was always wriggling out of my hands like a fish you thought you had all hooked and ready to pop in the pan. Was there ever a day I didn't at one point say, "Hey, when will life end?" Flashback! A new scene starring the boy who would soon be murdered.

BERT, *a fourteen-year-old kid, swaggers on, wearing earphones. He dances to silent music.*

ROSALIE: This scene you are about to see contains information completely unknown to the boy's mother, my sister. Information unknown to Captain Marvin Holahan of the Sixth Precinct Homicide. Those two people in the course of their lives never learned the information you are about to receive right now. This scene takes place in the Parthenon. Not the one in Greece that's the cradle of all civilization. Hell, baby, I'm talking the Parthenon Luncheonette on West Eleventh Street and Bleecker in Greenwich Village. This scene takes place four weeks before this boy, my nephew, will be murdered.

A booth and table and chairs come in. BERT *sits in the booth, his arm around one of the girls. Another boy,* DONNY, *has his sleeves rolled up and is wearing a lot of wristwatches. The girls lean forward. The kids are roughly twelve, thirteen, fourteen.*

BERT: It's so easy.
DONNY: Easy he says.
BERT: You stand on Christopher Street.
DONNY: I got to wait in the tub.

BERT: Pretty soon the guy stops.

DONNY: The tub gets cold. You got a cold ass waiting in the tub.

BERT: You noticed him cause he's walked back and forth a few times looking at you.

DONNY: All the things a tub can be. A coffin. I pretend I'm in a coffin.

JOANNE: Does he look at you like you're a girl?

DONNY: I pretend I'm in a boat.

JOANNE: Do they really look fruity?

BERT: Sometimes they're in cars. Not fruity cars, but Pontiacs. Oldsmobiles.

JOANNE: Fruits driving Pontiacs?

DONNY: I pretend I'm in a car.

MARGIE: I could see a Chevrolet. Chevrolets are fruity.

BERT: Not the '65 Chevy, Joanne. Holy shit, Joanne, I look at you sometimes and I say—

JOANNE: It was Margie who said it.

BERT: You were looking at her, agreeing with her.

JOANNE: Don't get mad at me. I'm sorry, Bert?

BERT: I don't like the two of you hanging around together. She's dragging you down. We all got to protect each other. Make each other better. Margie's dragging you down.

JOANNE: She's not cheap.

MARGIE: I only felt cheap once in my life. Charlie Ebbermann said he'd give me ten cents to let him touch me in the cloakroom. This is the fifth grade. The sixth grade. So I do. Big deal. Then I hear later, Charlie Ebbermann is paying a girl from the public school a quarter to take out her glass eye and let him look in. I saw him and I said Look, Ebbermann, you can take your dime back and I threw it at him.

BERT *calls:* Hey, could we get a Coke or something? A toasted bran?

DONNY: Bert brings the fruit upstairs. His mother's away. He leads them into the bathroom. I'm happy cause I can finally get out of the fucking tub. I hear the voices behind the shower curtain. I make sure the shower curtain's shut. I see the fruit's shadow on the shower curtain. I leap out of the tub and bang the guy on the head with the monkey wrench. He don't know what hit him.

BERT: I pull the watch off. Take the wallet. We roll 'em to the door. Push 'em out in the hall. We piss in the corner.

DONNY: Piss on the guy.

BERT: Then I knock on the door next door. Mrs. Pantoni, I tell her, there's another drunk broke in. He peed on the floor. I spill some wine on him. She calls the cops. The cops come and clear the guy out.

MARGIE: They don't ever report you?

BERT: You don't have big ears, but you're a real dumbo, Margie. I don't want you hanging around with her, Joanne.

JOANNE: I got to have some friends, Bert.

BERT: You got me.

JOANNE: You swear?

BERT, *with his arm around Joanne:* Who they gonna report? Some fairy tries to pick up a fourteen-year-old?

JOANNE: All that ticking. Your arm is so noisy.

DONNY: You have all the fun. I got to stick in the tub. You wait in the tub for a while. You see how much fun it is in a fucking tub.

BERT: Some fairy in a Chevrolet with Jersey plates is gonna pick you up? I want to make some money, not scare 'em away.

DONNY: That's right. I'd scare 'em away. *He makes a face.*

JOANNE: Let me wind your watches? You read in the papers

today about the lady in Forest Hills who died and they couldn't figure out how she died? She was healthy. Well, you know how she died?

BERT: Donny hit her over the head with his monkey.

DONNY: That's right. I hit her over the head with my monkey.

MARGIE: Would you let her tell her story?

BERT *calls:* You burning that bran muffin?

JOANNE: She had this beautiful beehive hairdo that she wore. Really intricate. Curls. Upswept. Spit curls. And she didn't want to damage it because her hairdo was really a work of art. *Hairdo Magazine* was considering her for a feature. And she kept spraying her hairdo with hair spray so her hairdo wouldn't get hurt when she went to sleep at night and you know what happened? In Forest Hills, Queens, they traced black widow spiders escaped and hid in her hair. Somehow they ended up in her hair because they like dark places and the hair spray made this shield like *Gardol* on the toothpaste commercial where the decay can't get through the toothpaste. And the black widow spiders got trapped within her hairdo in this wall of hair spray and got panicked and couldn't get out and ate their way through her skull. Bit her in the skull to get out and that's how she died.

BERT *and* JOANNE *neck.*

DONNY: Bert?

MARGIE: Can I have a bite of that bran muffin?

DONNY: Bert? Is your mother at work?

JOANNE: Bran is supposed to be the secret of life.

BERT: You feel like getting another wrist watch?

MARGIE: How'd that woman do her hair?

BERT *and* DONNY *get up and go.* JOANNE *begins demonstrating.
The lights come down on the luncheonette . . . a fanfare of
music. The lights come up on* ROSALIE, *by her piano. She pre-
pares herself for the next scene, putting on a red kimono.*

ROSALIE: Flashback. Eighteen months ago. I was still among
the living. How my sister and nephew came to New York
in the first place.

The lights come up on Rosalie's apartment. ROSALIE *moves into
the scene. The apartment contains a sink, a table, a chair, a
day bed strewn with clothes, a vanity.* ROSALIE'S *waking up
and putting on make-up and drinking coffee and looking in
the mirror.* BETTY *looks different from what we have seen
before. Two years ago, she was very plain. Very nervous.*

BETTY: Rosalie, you got to come home. You're growing up not
knowing your family. Your nephew. Our mother. BERT
shyly looks out from under his mother's arm.
ROSALIE: Hiya, kid. Want a snort?
BETTY: Tell her, Bert.
BERT: Bangor, Maine, is about the greatest place I know. It's
not like the old days when nothing was there. Bangor,
Maine, is the home of one of the world's busiest airports.
He holds out a pennant marked "Bangor."
ROSALIE: He's great.
BERT: Bangor, Maine, is the center of the chartered jet service
that takes Americans to all parts of the globe on budget
flights.
ROSALIE: You done good, Betty.
BETTY: Rosalie, Bangor is so interesting. You meet people from
all over the world who are laying over. Lots of times

they're fogged in and you get to hear about their travels and I sell souvenirs and there's an opening in the cocktail lounge. You could sing. You'd meet such interesting people. I pray for snow. I pray for fog. All the things that used to make life so dismal in Bangor are now the exact things that make it so interesting.

ROSALIE: Honeybunch, you're hearing about the world. But hearing about don't put no notches on anyone's pistol. I'm doing. Bert, would you go out onto Christopher Street to the Li-Lac Chocolate store and request about a pound of kisses? *She gives Bert money.* BERT *goes.*

BETTY: Bert, you be careful. Is it safe out there?

ROSALIE: Honeybunch, I get this call last week, would I be interested appearing in a film. Sure, why not.

BETTY: He's never been to a city before.

ROSALIE: I report to a motel on Forty-Second Street and Eleventh Avenue. Way west. Take elevator to the sixth floor. Knock. Go in. Floodlights. A camera. Workmen setting up. The real thing! A man said, "You the girl? Get your duds off. Sink into the feathers and go to it." Holy shit, they're loading the cameras and I'm naked and nobody's really paying attention. They say, "You all set?" Sure, why not. Lights. Camera. Action. And a door I thought was a closet opens up and it's from another room and a gorilla leaps out with a slit in his suit and this enormous erection and the gorilla jumps on me. Honeybunch, there's no surprises like that in Maine. And we're going at it and I can't believe it and after about five minooties, the director yells "Cut!" and the gorilla rolls off me, takes off his gorilla head and it's Harry Reems from *Deep Throat* and *The Devil in Miss Jones*. What an honor to meet you, sir, I said. Christ! Go back to Bangor, Maine!

Honey, you should move in with me. Get yourself un-
saddled from Momma and that house and airports.

BETTY: It's our family.

ROSALIE: Honeybaby, start your own family. I started my own
family. I've got a family motto. She Travels Fastest Who
Travels Alone. I live here on Christopher Street. A lovely
building. Lovely neighbors. Leave you alone. Nobody
knows me. I don't know anybody. I'm flying high. I'm
working for a travel agency. Dawn's Promising Star
Travel Agency. Founder and sponsor of Honeymoon
Holidays. No charter jets for me. When I travel, which
shall be soon, I'll be traveling First Class not out of
Bangor, but right out of old JFK. Wait till you meet my
boss, Raulito. Take it back. Erase those tapes. You'll never
meet him. I'd show you my life, you'd get so jealous,
you'd want to move right in and take me over. You can't
have me. You can have yourself but you can't have me.
Ditch the kid. He comes from a whole other rotten period
of your life. Erase those tapes. Get rid of him. I got a pull-
out sofa. Move in. We can have some laughs.

BETTY: I've got lots of laughs in Bangor. When it isn't raining,
it's snowing. I meet boys at the airport, but they end up
taking planes. Momma sits by the TV singing "Rosalie,
My Darling." Aside from that, everything's okay.

ROSALIE: Listen, send the kid back. There's an extra key.

BETTY: Momma sent me down here to bring you back.

ROSALIE: You just wire a little wire to Momma. Hey, Momma,
send me a change-of-address card. I get lonely, Honeybunch. We could have some laughs. I'm proud of my life
and I'd like to show it off to you. We're young.

BERT *enters with a box of chocolates.*

ROSALIE: Hiya, kid. We were just talking about you.
BERT: Kisses!

The lights go out on Bert and Betty in Rosalie's apartment.
ROSALIE *whips off her bathrobe and steps in time to the very
jazzy piano music. Behind the stage is bare, black. A cyclist
wearing a mask, goggles, helmet, and shorts appears upstage,
holding a bicycle over his head. As* ROSALIE *speaks to us, he
advances slowly, threateningly, toward her.*

ROSALIE: So I walk out on Christopher, cut down on Bleecker
    to walk to work and I'm just jazzing along Hudson
    Street, and you know where that Ristorante Rigoletto is
    that the papers gave eighteen tureens to and they got lim-
    ousines parked out front and I happen to know the chef
    sprays fresh herbs on the canned Boyardee, but, what the
    hell, it's over-priced, out of the way, they treat you like
    shit, and Uptown loves it. Well, I'm being so specific be-
    cause it's just at that very location that a ten-speed yellow
    Raleigh bike bears down on me. I apparently splattered
    up against the window of the Ristorante Rigoletto like a
    pizza that suddenly appeared on the menu. My last
    thoughts were of Betty moving down to New York. I won
    her. Revenge on our Momma. I was feeling very happy.

The sound of a crash. ROSALIE *shrugs her shoulders and goes
into the dark. The* MASKED MAN *glares at us, never lowering
his bicycle.*

MASKED MAN: I don't give a shit if she's dead! Who's gonna fix
    my bike? The chain is off my bike! Who's gonna pay for
    that? Give me her bag. She owes me money. Life belongs
    to the living. I don't give a shit if she just died. She

should've looked. I am traveling. I am moving. Who's
gonna pay for my bike? Chocolate? That's all she's got
in the fucking bag? Chocolate kisses? How am I supposed to fix my bike with chocolate kisses? She deserves
to die. *He walks off into the black.*

The lights come up on ROSALIE, *who sits by the piano and
sings.*

ROSALIE:

Was that Mister Right?
If it was, I'll let it pass.
The right Mister Right
That funky looking skunk put me kerplunk on my ass
I thought Mister Right
Would have a little more couth.
He'd come on a white charger
Say Hi-de-hi to my charm
And Vo-de-oh to my youth.

The bright jazz tune plays.

ROSALIE: So Betty Yearn, newly arrived from Bangor, Maine,
stays in New York to settle my estate along with my hash.
She moves into my apartment, she takes over my job. I'm
not even cool in the grave yet, and she's got my job. She
moves into my life. Betty Yearns's first day eighteen
months ago in the Dawn's Promising Star Travel Agency.
A division of Honeymoon Holidays.

*The jazz music turns Latin. The lights come up on the travel
agency: a desk, a telephone, lots of telephone books, a cassette*

recorder that contains tapes of cheering and applause. BETTY *is
dressed in a pretty outfit for her first day at work. And if she
can wear pants and look pretty,* RAULITO *can wear what appears to be—is it?—a gold lamé evening gown over his business suit, and still look mucho macho. Raulito is very
handsome, like a 1940's Latin leading man with a pompadour
and diamond rings. He carries an armful of Sunday's papers.
He is sexually very threatening.*

RAULITO: You take the *Daily News.* You take the *Sunday
Times.* Not the financial section. Not the sports section.

BETTY: There's so many sections.

RAULITO: The engagement section.

BETTY: The society page.

RAULITO: You look up the name of the father, the man who is
paying for the wedding.

BETTY: Mr. and Mrs. Bernard Culkin of Corona and Point
Lookout announce the engagement of their daughter,
Lillibet—

RAULITO: Stop right there. You look in the phone book. Not
the Manhattan phone book.

BETTY: So I look up Corona in . . . there are so many phone
books. I've only been here a few days.

RAULITO: Corona is in Queens.

BETTY: Culkin. BBBBBB Bernard.

RAULITO: Don't *show* it to me. Copy the phone number down
on the pad.

BETTY: I swear to you, I'm generally very good at writing
numbers.

RAULITO: Check the bride-to-be's name.

BETTY: Lillibet.

RAULITO: See what Lillibet does? Where Lillibet is employed.

BETTY: Educated at St. John's University.

RAULITO: Your sister was like streaks of lightning here.

BETTY: Is employed as a researcher at Mutual Life.

RAULITO: So she should be home at five thirty. Mark down to call her at?

BETTY: Five forty-five?

RAULITO: Five thirty-one!

BETTY: Nice to have a few minutes to get your coat off.

RAULITO: Your late and more and more lamented sister would have that phone ringing off the hook the instant Lillibet Culkin Corona Queens stuck her key in the door.

BETTY: Fine.

RAULITO: If I may be so bold, petals on a pool drifting, you want a travel brochure back to Bangor?

BETTY: No! I feel my sister wanted me to have this job.

RAULITO: No hard feelings. We can be friends. If I'm ever in Bangor, God forbid, I'll look you up. Is the job too hard for you?

BETTY: I can do it.

RAULITO: Then, honey through the comb sifting, you must be prepared to play Follow the Leader. Miss Lisa Staminelli to wed law student. Bayside, Queens. Father Frank Staminelli. Presented to society the Gotham Ball. You have the Queens phone book. Zut zut zut zut *zutt* you have the number. You dial it. *He accomplishes this task in a brilliant quick stroke.* This is where my Rosalie was brilliant. *He talks into the phone.* Miss Lisa Staminelli. Is she there? Is this she? This is she? The noted debutante? I am talking to her. Ohhhhh, Miss Staminelli, this is *Bride's Magazine* calling. Of course I'm breathless. Are you sitting down? Miss Staminelli, you've won our lottery. An all-expense-paid honeymoon for two to Paradise Cove. Two weeks!

BETTY: Two weeks?

RAULITO: Yes! For you and Mr. Right— *He checks the paper.* Bruce Mandrake. How did I know? Darling, we here at *Bride's Magazine* know *tout!* If we didn't know who was getting married, we wouldn't know if the world would keep spinning. We need families and families are love and love pulled your number out of the lottery. Fate wanted you and your new husband, Mr. Mandrake—is he the magician?—to have this honeymoon. Do you think it's possible, God, we know you're so busy. Would it be possible for you and Señor Right to stop down to our office to pick up your honeymoon? Fourteenth Street. 618 West. Ninth floor. The Honeymoon Holidays Building. Could you and Bruce toddle on down here any night after work, say seven? We could finalize arrangements for the honeymoon? Some forms to sign. *The piano plays a tango.* Then you could have a lovely evening in the Village. Greenwich Village. Chianti. Pasta. Discuss your future. Discuss your honeymoon. It's all luck and love is luck and you're the luckiest girl in the world, Lisa. The past shows us the mistakes we made. The future's the place where we won't make them again. Dreams are the fuel for reality. A new family is coming into the world! Oh God! Grab the Now! The Now is all quicksilver and mercury. The Now is diamonds. Can I make an appointment for you? *The music stops.* Lucky you! I could squeeze you in tomorrow at seven ten. Oh, Lisa, you've made all of us so happy at *Bride's Magazine. He puts on a cassette of cheering.* See you tomorrow. *He hangs up.* You're the bait, baby. You lure them in here. *You* decorate the hook. *I* make the sale.

BETTY: Everybody falls for it?

RAULITO: Sometimes a black eye. Every now and then a death

threat. But, Sweetness and Light, if I can make one sale
a week, that is two trips to the Caribbean, I can make out
all right. Besides what is living without a little danger?

BETTY: Do they ever call *Bride's Magazine*?

RAULITO: Only the smart ones and they're not exactly our
clientele.

BETTY: Could we be sued?

RAULITO: By who?

BETTY: *Bride's Magazine*.

RAULITO: For what?

BETTY: I don't want to go to jail. My life is beginning. I don't
want to be arrested.

RAULITO: Hey, hey, hey. Evidence obtained by wiretap is il-
legal. Can't be introduced into court. What planet you
from anyway, baby?

BETTY: What borough is the moon in?

RAULITO: The moon is the fifty-first state. Hawaii. Alaska. The
moon. Did you see the moon last night? Like a little
Turkish flag waving in the sky? I saluted.

BETTY: Why do you dress that way?

RAULITO: That is exactly what your sister Rosalie said to me
the first time we met. We would curl up on her pull-out
sleep sofa, now *your* pull-out sleep sofa, and I would tell
her my dream to one night turn on the TV and hear the
Late Show say, "And tonight our guest is ME!" *He puts
on a cassette of people cheering.* Thank you Johnny. I'm
from Cuba. We lived on the other side of the island. From
Havana.

The piano plays Latin-style. RAULITO *sits beside the desk as if
he were the guest on the "Tonight Show" and Betty were the
host.*

RAULITO: Poor. You never saw such poor. We were so poor *that*. You know those jokes? He was so fat *that*. She was so dumb *that*. Well, we were so *poor* that. When I was wearing rags, I was running around naked. This part of Cuba that we called the country, I think any normal thinking person would call it the jungle. Occasionally, a magazine would appear in our village and I'd see the pictures of evening gowns and spangles and barrettes in the hair and these high heels. I didn't know till later that was what women wore. I thought that was rich people. I thought if you were rich and lived in the city or lived in America that was what the average American family hung around in. The Revolution came. I saw Che Guevara this close. We left Cuba. We got to Florida. Where I found out that those uniforms with diamonds and lace did not belong to the typical American man. But a few years ago, I was shopping in the Salvation Army for a winter coat and I came upon this real Rita Hayworth special. A beautiful 1940's evening gown for twenty-five cents. I bought it. Why not? The dreams we have as kids, they're the dreams we never get over. I put it on over my suit. I feel rich. I feel successful.

RAULITO *begins to spin so the dress flares out. He advances seductively on Betty, now waving his dress like a matador's cape in front of her.* BETTY *is terrified.* RAULITO *shows no mercy.*

RAULITO: I feel I can get out of the jungle and get to America and twirl and twirl. Feeling good outside I start to feel good inside. I start Honeymoon Holidays. I want to start a family. I want to start a life. Betty, your sister went with

me. Your sister would let me dance with her first. Then
she would let me sleep with her after and dreams would
come out of our heads like little Turkish moons. We
would salute. Betty?

BETTY, *getting back to work:* It's about five thirty. I'd better
call Lillibet.

RAULITO: You like the name Lillibet?

BETTY: It's a name. People have names. I take the Queens
phone book.

RAULITO: Do you know what Queen Elizabeth's secret name
is? If you were in her royal family what you would call
her?

BETTY: Elizabeth. They'd call her Elizabeth. They'd call her
Queen Elizabeth. Elizabeth is short for Queen Elizabeth.

RAULITO: They'd call her Lillibet.

BETTY: I thought I was safe when I came in here, when I met
you at my sister's funeral I thought, this guy's a weirdo but
I'll be safe.

RAULITO: Lillibet is the Queen's secret name. What Prince
Philip calls her when they're alone. I read that in *People's*
magazine. Alone must mean also in the royal bed. Prince
Philip calls over to her: Lillibet? He turns on the royal
radio station. A little English Latin music comes on the
Royal Radio. I should call you Lillibet. Tell me your
story? Unfold yourself to me?

BETTY: I'm Betty. Betty's short for Elizabeth. I'm a Betty.
That's all I am. I have no story. I'm no guest on any talk
show. No story. I am a middle-aged woman. I'm a young
girl. I'm regular. Quiet. Normal. Human person. *She is
shaking violently. She puts on the cheering on the cassette
and dials the telephone.* Is Miss Lillibet Culkin there? Hi!
This is *Bride's Magazine* calling. The lottery of love

twirled and stopped at . . . oh? The wedding is off? The
groom is dead? Head injuries? Attacked by a monkey
wrench? Greenwich Village? Beaten brutally? Watch
stolen? I don't care. Don't tell me your troubles. You won
a honeymoon. That's all I want to tell you. That's all. *She
hangs up.* Lillibet Culkin. Corona, Queens. I don't want
the job. I can't handle the job. I'm not my sister. I am not
Rosalie. I can't do her job. I'm not Lillibet. I'm not Queen
Elizabeth. I'm nobody. I'm me. I can't do the job. I don't
want the job.

RAULITO *has picked her up. He tangos her away into the dark.*
ROSALIE *appears by the piano. She sings while the travel agency
is being replaced by the apartment.*

ROSALIE:

>
> Frightened of you
> All of these years
> Never secure
> In your embrace
> Sleep through the night
> Dream that I'm dead
> Feeling your weight
> There in the bed
> One little bag
> Never unpacked
> Hidden away
> In case
> I get the nerve
> One day to leave
> Finally that fact
> To face

What's getting me through my life?
What's my excuse inside?
What's keeping me in my life?
The molehill of lust or the mountain of pride?
Forgive me, my dear
A slip of the tongue
Forget what I said
Erase
I meant to say
My life is brightened by you
The darkness whitened by you
Each moment heightened by you
My life enlightened by you
But not I'm frightened of you
Forgive me
I'm sorry
Don't hit me
I love you

A year and a half later. Eighteen count 'em eighteen
months. My sister has moved into my life. It's like two
days before the boy's murder.

The lights upstage show BETTY *and* RAULITO *necking, passion-
ately. He has gathered his evening gown up under the trench
coat he now wears.* BETTY *is quite snappily dressed and a lot
more sure of herself in the last months since we've seen her.
The music is ominous.* ROSALIE *goes into the black.* RAULITO
*kisses Betty one time more, and he goes into the dark. The
lights come up on the apartment.* BERT *sits on a red beanbag
winding watches. He tenses.* BETTY *straightens herself. She
comes in the room. She begins to take off her dress and put on
a robe.*

BETTY: I bought this new dress today. You like it? *She takes another dress out of a paper bag.* Or do you like this one? What do you think moving maybe to Miami? I got a chance finally after eighteen months at Raulito's. A free trip for two. National Airlines. There's a lot of cities we could fly to. L.A. Round-trip ticket but we could just stay. Stop winding all those watches. I never saw anyone for finding so many watches. Find 'em and wind 'em. That's your name. The watch monster. That's what I gave birth to. Can't you say anything? Jesus. Who'd've thought you'd grow up to be your father. To have to live through all that again. Can't you say anything?

BERT: How's Honeymoon Holidays?

BETTY: Raulito called me a professional today. He gave me a gold star. *She picks up the phone.* Miss Mary Louise Nicholson? The lottery of love twirled and twirled and stopped at your number. It don't hurt to start a marriage with a good honeymoon. *She slams the phone down.*

BERT: Did you and Daddy have a good honeymoon?

BETTY: If I had a good honeymoon, you think I'd be working at Honeymoon Holidays?

BERT: You going to marry Raulito?

BETTY: Raulito already has a wife and about nineteen children. He gave me this butterfly pin. It was his grandmother's. *She bends it.* Now you bend it. I don't want anybody doing nice for me. BERT *bends the pin.* BETTY *throws the pin away.* I don't want anybody giving me presents. I don't want to be reminded what I missed out on. We should've had a family. We could've had a family. A regular dynasty. I had a family. I should've passed one on to you. If we'd had a family, we'd go to the movies and eat at McDonald's and take summer trips to Maine to see

your grandmother and see free Shakespeare in the park
and take long rides on the subway to the Bronx Zoo and
the Brooklyn Botanicals. If we had a family, things'd be a
lot different around here.

BERT: Why can't we do all those things now? They're all free.

BETTY: Because they're things families do together. Because
they remind me how I screwed up my life. If we don't do
nothing, I don't get reminded. But I don't want to turn
you against your father. I want you to love your father.
Your father was a god. Your father was the handsomest
man I ever saw. Your father had a body you could see
through his clothes. Your father had shoulders out to here
and a waist you could clasp your thumb and index finger
around. A brain of a fucking wizard. He could remember
telephone numbers. Addresses. He could remember lottery numbers and the social security numbers of people
he met a hundred years ago. Serial numbers of guys he
was in the Army with. He was kind of creepy when you
come to think of it.

BERT: He sounds great.

BETTY: We bumped into an old Army buddy and your father
said "I remember you. 19769982." The guy says "Hey,
why'd you remember my serial number?" Your father
says "Hold on. I haven't been thinking about you all these
years. I just happen to have that kind of memory."

BERT: So why's he forgot where we live?

BETTY: A blind spot. He forgot you. He forgot me. For a guy
with a memory. What I think is us living on Christopher
Street. Ever since the Catholic Church said St. Christopher
doesn't exist, maybe he thinks Christopher Street doesn't
exist either.

BERT: But you left him.

BETTY: I didn't mind him, well, I did, him putting my head down the toilet and flushing it. But you. When he put your head down the toilet and flushed it, I said that's it. And I told him to leave.

BERT: I have dreams sometimes of water rushing by me.

BETTY: That comes from your father putting your head down the toilet.

BERT: I think I'll join the Navy when I can. The submarine service.

BETTY: You been seeing too many Walt Disney movies.

JOANNE *runs in, breathless:* You know what my mother told me today? A lady in her office knew a lady who died and they couldn't find a reason why she died. She was healthy.

BETTY: I don't want to hear any more black widow spiders. You get me?

JOANNE: This isn't black widow spiders. This is the truth. This lady died and they traced all her steps and they found she had gone to Korvette's Department Store and on her dead body they found her wearing a beautiful Indian blouse with pieces of mirror sewn in it.

BETTY: Sounds pretty. Korvette's?

JOANNE: And they traced all her steps and went to Korvette's and opened the drawer where the Indian blouses came from and they reached in and the detective pulled back his hand because it almost got bit by a cobra. Which is what happened to the lady. These blouses had come in from India. And cobra eggs had got woven in beneath the mirrors while the blouses were being made and the cobra eggs hatched from the heat of being mailed over here and the lady reached her hand in the drawer and got bitten and died.

BETTY *serves Bert dinner.* BERT *eats.*

BETTY: Where is this woman? How come you always have these friends who are getting bit by black widow spiders? Bit by cobras.

BERT: It was her mother's friend.

BETTY: I don't believe her mother.

BERT: Then you don't believe me. Are you calling me a liar?

BETTY: I don't want you hanging around together. I don't want any more stories about black widow spiders and black widow cobras. I'm up to here with it. JOANNE *runs out.* And you be careful with her. I don't want any fourteen-year-old fathers living in my house. I'm not ready to be a grandmother yet.

BERT: You old hag. You old crone. I know how old you are. You're thirty-six and you're gonna die soon and I'm fourteen and I'm going to live forever. I hate you. You're going to die. You know what I want for Christmas? You in a coffin under a Christmas tree. Why did Aunt Rosalie have to die? Why couldn't you be the one that bicycle hit. Maybe that guy is around right now speeding down streets looking for you.

BETTY: You know why you can't hurt me? Cause I have X-ray eyes and I can see right into your heart.

BERT: Bullshit.

BETTY: Remember that old man with the pushcart in Bangor who called out "OLD CLOTHES"? You used to follow him for hours. What did you do with that filthy old man? Old Clothes. I place my X-ray eyes over you and I see deep in you Old Clothes. Old Clothes. Old Clothes.

BERT: Don't say that.

BETTY: Old clothes. Old rags. Old rats. X-ray eyes.

BERT: Don't say that! Don't say that!

BETTY: Don't have to say it. I feel it. I'm being very quiet and saying to myself over and over. *Wordless:* Old clothes.

BERT *hits her. She hits him back.*

BERT: Shut up! Shut up!

BETTY: I'm not saying anything. *Wordless:* Old clothes.

BERT: It's what you're thinking. Can't think that. Stop! Stop!

BETTY: I love thinking. I can think anything I want.

BERT: I've killed people.

BETTY: Don't make me laugh.

BERT: I haven't killed them. Donny's killed them.

BETTY: There you are. You couldn't hurt a fly. I do not mean that as a compliment. I mean that as a truth. You could not wound a mosquito. If David and Goliath had a fight, Goliath would reach down and squeeze your head like a seedless grape.

BERT: I lure them up here while you're away and Donny and I kill them. Hit them on the head with the monkey. Take their watches. Roll them out in the hall. They don't dare call the cops on us. I can so hurt a fly.

BETTY *slaps him:* Lure? Where'd you learn a word like lure?

BERT: I know a lot of words.

BETTY: There's a whole series of murders going around.

BERT: Maybe that's me.

BETTY: Decapitations.

BERT: What's that?

BETTY: Down at all these rough bars down by the river, Raulito told me at work they find people with heads chopped off. The police don't bother to check them out. It's not worth the trouble. You're not part of those murders, are you? I told you to stay away from those docks, you little faggot.

BERT: What's decap—decap—

BETTY: Chop their heads off!

BERT: I didn't do that! I swear! I'm just into watches. Money.

The monkey wrench. I don't think any of them ever died.
I swear.

A MAN *appears at the door—a large man, carefully dressed in
a white linen suit, Panama hat, and black string tie. He carries
flowers.*

BETTY: Yes?

MAN: Betty? Betty Mandible?

BETTY: I was.

BERT: Are you the police?

MAN: You got married.

BETTY: Oh yes. My husband here and I are very happy. Some
people say he's too young. I say why not?

MAN: Hello, Betty.

BERT: My mother says go away. She doesn't know you. Ma? Is
this guy bothering you?

BETTY: I know who you are.

MAN: I was hoping you would.

BETTY: In Bangor. Summer of—

MAN: Nineteen years ago. I'm Durwood Peach.

BETTY: Durwood Peach. The Good Humor Man. Pushing that
white ice-cream truck.

DURWOOD: Name like a flavor ice cream. The special may be
blueberry ripple but I'm pushing the peach.

BETTY: You were from North—

DURWOOD: South.

BETTY: Carolina. You came up to Bangor, to visit your aunt.

DURWOOD: Can I sit down for a minute? Excuse me for not
being on my toes more. Oh, I have been driving. I drove
from South Carolina straight up to Bangor, Maine, and
looked up your name in the phone book. Your mother

answered. She told me your swell sister had passed on.
She told me you were here. You were the one I wanted. I
got back in my car and drove from Maine nonstop here to
Christopher Street. So this is Greenwich Village. Sure is
lively. Mexican restaurant and a Chinese restaurant and
an Indian restaurant all on one block. A lot of variety.
Your mother didn't mention you had a little boy. Is he
yours?

BERT: I'm hers.

BETTY: Why are you here?

DURWOOD: See. Now I should said that soon as I arrived. I
never forgot you nineteen years ago and even though we
never talked much and you had other boyfriends and you
and me never went out, I have recently realized you are
the only girl I ever loved, ever will love. My doctor gave
me a note saying all this was true.

BETTY: Doctor?

DURWOOD: I been in a hospital and I got out and I been going
to a doctor and you appeared to me like a holy movie
when the Blessed Virgin appears and tells the holy children what to do. You appeared in my analysis. Here's the
note.

BETTY: Thank you. *She takes the note.*

DURWOOD: Now my knees are shaking. I'm gonna faint.

BERT: Should I call the police?

DURWOOD: No! I'm all right. It's all the driving from South
Carolina to Bangor, Maine, back to New York. Betty, I
love you. I'll always love you. I've never loved anyone
else. I've told my wife. She understands. She's written a
note to you giving me up to you.

BETTY *reads:* "Dear Betty. I surrender all rights to Durwood
heartbroken and bereft as that leaves me."

DURWOOD: My grandfather, the only surviving member of my
natural family, the head of the clan, welcomes you into
the family. I'm rich, Betty. I've got a farm and I lease it
out to a racetrack and I make lots of money. Here's a
thousand dollars in single new bills as a sign of faith. You
remember me. I didn't have to introduce myself. I thought
I'd have to introduce myself. That's a good sign. You remember me.

BERT: You want me to get my monkey? Bang him down on
his head? I can get Donny down here.

BETTY: I never even kissed you.

DURWOOD: To pursue the unattainable. My doctor says that's
my problem.

BETTY: The unattainable I'm afraid I must remain.

DURWOOD: No, you won't. I won't lie to you. I have been sick.
And to be cured, I must once in my life obtain the unob-
tainable or I will die. I'm staying at the Dixie Hotel on
West Forty-Second Street. I'll return there now and leave
this one thousand dollars to show my good faith. I'll leave
these photos of my farm and all that you'll be mistress of.
A mountain. A river. Caves that are closed to the public.
I'll give you time to peruse my offer and would like to
ask your permission to call tomorrow night after which
time perhaps we could leave immediately. You cannot
escape from me or the power of my mind. We will begin
a family. I'll be cured. We'll be happy. All these years. I'll
be back tomorrow evening at six P.M. with my bags
packed. I'll make a reservation at the Mexican restaurant
for two.

BERT: For three.

DURWOOD: For two, Betty. You and me.

BETTY: I don't think you need reservations at Taco Trolley.

DURWOOD: Until tomorrow, Betty. Your mother's angry at you. She said she sent you down here to bring your sister back and you never returned. She said she had messages for you. She said get in touch. If I can bring you together, you and your mother, that'll be doing good. My doctor will be so happy. He said if you really want her, you'll find her. I didn't have to call. You were home. One of the largest cities in the world. You were here. Now I'm here. I'll be back tomorrow. The special is blueberry. But I'm pushing the peach.

DURWOOD *goes.* BERT *has been counting the money Durwood left behind.*

BETTY: I got to sit down.
BERT: You think it's counterfeit? You bend the face in half on two bills and if they fit together, the two faces into one face, that proves it's not counterfeit.
BETTY: I remember him.
BERT: You must've been the prettiest girl around that summer.
BETTY: I was pretty. But not this pretty. Do you think he's telling the truth? South Carolina? Should I go? Maybe he does have money. Get us out of here. Who cares if he's a nut. It's amazing how a little tomorrow can make up for a whole lot of yesterday. It sounds like one of those uplift songs in a musical comedy. *She sings:* "It's amazing how a little tomorrow."
BERT *sings:* "Makes up for a whole lot of yesterday."
BETTY: "It's amazing how a little tomorrow." Do you have a joint? A jay? Don't do lies to me. I found them in the Saltine box the last time.
BERT: This time I hid the dope in the one place you'd never look.

BETTY: Stop making with the funnies . . . I want to keep this
   moment. I feel it going away already and I'm hanging
   on to it. Don't go away, magic moment. I'll be right there.
BERT: The one place you'd never look.
BETTY: I give up.
BERT: The broom closet.
BETTY: You're right. The one place I'd never look. I like giant
   dustballs. It gives me a flavor of the Old West.

*They sit on the day bed and light up. The lights dim slightly
on them as they smoke.* ROSALIE *and her piano appear in the
light at left.* ROSALIE *sings it like one of those rousing uplift
songs in a musical comedy.*

ROSALIE:

> It's amazing how a little tomorrow
> Can make up for a whole lot of yesterday
> It's amazing how a little tomorrow
> Can make up for a whole lot of yesterday
> Yesterday was dreary
> Clocks kept on crawling
> Now the future's cheery
> How thrilling, how enthralling
> It's amazing how a little tomorrow
> Can recompense an awful lot of sorrow
> So get yourself a little tomorrow
> And wake up from those awful yesterdays.
> Shake up all those bore-filled yester—
> Make up those unlawful yesterdays.

*She dances back to the piano, bows and goes into the dark-
ness.* BERT *and* BETTY *sit on the day bed.*

BETTY: The first time I ever smoked pot, I was in a bar in Rhode Island with my girlfriend.

BERT, *bombed by the joint:* The summer you met Durwood?

BETTY: No, after. This guy asked us if we wanted to smoke reefers and my girlfriend said "Only if you promise we'll turn into sex-crazed nymphomaniacs who won't be held responsible for any of their activities." *A* MAN *appears upstage in the light, dressed like a beatnik.* And the man said . . .

MAN, *striking a match:* Results guaranteed.

BETTY: And off we went. He had a car.

MAN, *lighting a cigarette:* Get in.

BETTY: What's that black rag?

MAN: I'm going to have to blindfold you girls seeing as how I am the Dope King of Providence, Rhode Island.

BETTY: Ooooo, I love an expert. Shut up, Betty. Just shut up.

DOPE KING: Look, you little twats, if you ever got caught, you couldn't reveal where I'd taken you. You couldn't betray me, but then I couldn't have you betray yourselves with the knowledge you knew where the dope headquarters of Providence, Rhode Island, was. I'm doing this for you, you little twats.

BETTY: We drove, the three of us, my girlfriend, him, me. We giggled suicidally because maybe this man steering his car right then left then left then right would murder us and if he did we should remember where he took us. I had heard that directions given before death stay embroidered on your brain and the police can use that for a clue. I didn't care if we were murdered. My life was beginning. There was a hit song that summer. We drove singing it. *She sings in a clear, pure voice:*

Hey Stay a While
In the crook of my arms
All you got to do is
Look in my arms
And you'll see Home Sweet Home
I'll invest in a doormat
Hey Home Sweet Home
We'll test the mattress
Our arms are sinuous
All performances are continuous
Hey Stay a While
Feel the smile in my arms
And the smile's in my arms
All for you
Sit back/Relax
Cool brow/Tension slacks
Hey Stay a While
My arms are filled with
What the whole world lacks
Hey Stay a While

Mavis, because that was my girlfriend's name, Mavis
Brennan is squeezing my hand and I'm squeezing hers.
Where are we? I smell bread. That Portuguese bakery.
I think I know where we are.

DOPE KING: We're here.

BETTY: He led us out of the car. We held hands like mountain
climbers. Doors open. Stairs climb.

MAN: Okay. Open your eyes.

BETTY: Three steps. One. Two. Three. Doors shut. It was the
room I had lived in the year before when I was working
in the shoe factory for the summer. I saw traces on the

wall where I had written "Fuck You" in peanut butter
the year before one night because here I was seventeen
and my life still hadn't begun and I'm out supporting
myself. I said "Is Miss Carter the landlady here? Is that
the shoe factory over there?" I said "Boy, some dope king.
Living in a seventeen-dollar-a-week rooming house with
breakfast thrown in on Saturday."

DOPE KING: Some breakfast.

The lights go off on the Dope King.

BETTY, *watching where he went:* We laughed and laughed.

BERT: That's nice. You go to a strange place and they take off
your blindfolders and it's a place where you lived.

BETTY: That is precisely what I did not, underline the not, did
not like. I remember Miss Carter had said, "What's that
word in peanut butter on the wall?" I said, "Oh, you
think that says Fuck? You dirty lady. That's a message
in speedwriting: If You See Kay. Kay was my girl
friend," I said. "If you see Kay, remind us both to rd ths
msj and gt a bttr jb." Memories within memories. I'm
remembering what I remembered in my memory...

BERT: Where's Mavis?

BETTY: She died or something.

BERT: Mavis Brennan.

BETTY: Don't be such a busybody.

BERT: Mavis Brennan.

BETTY: What am I telling you stories about dope for? I should
be telling you stories how I didn't take dope. I should be
a father influence to you.

BERT: How did you die?

BETTY: Who died?

BERT: Mavis Brennan.

BETTY: Don't be so morbid. I didn't say she died.

BERT: You said she died.

BETTY: Or something.

BERT: What's the something?

BETTY: You lose touch. Touch gets lost.

BERT: Will I lose touch with you?

BETTY: You're my kid. You're me. You're the fruit of my loins
or the fruit of my loom. Some joke Mavis and I used to
make about phrases in the Bible. Jesus came riding into
town on his ass. We'd laugh. I wish sometimes you were
a girl. I wish sometimes I had a friend. Mavis Brennan.

BERT: You can call me Mavis.

BETTY: Mavis, I'm in love with a boy named Bert.

BERT: Do you love him a lot?

BETTY: More than life itself.

BERT: Do you love life?

BETTY: More than Bert himself.

BERT: Do you love me?

BETTY: But Mavis, you're my best friend.

BERT: Can I rub your hair?

BETTY *sits at the kitchen table:* Oh, yes, Mavis.

BERT *rubs her hair:* When I rub your hair, I can feel the oil
from it under my fingernails. I sit in class and the teacher
says "Get your fingers out of your nose." He says "You
can always tell the Catholic kids from the Protestant kids."
He says "The Catholic kids are always picking their nose
and the Protestant kids are always biting their nails." He's
bald and he says "Grass doesn't grow on busy streets."

BETTY: You tell him grass doesn't grow on rocks either. This
feels so good . . . don't stop . . . Bert . . . Mavis . . .

BERT *goes to the sink, gets a tray containing basin, pitcher,
water, and shampoo:* I'm getting the basin.

BETTY: I washed my hair last night.

BERT: Let me wash it tonight? Please? Momma, we have a thousand dollars in bills of consecutive numbers. You are loved. You have decisions to make. Momma, let me clear your head. You always think better when I wash your hair.

He pours water over her hair. She leans back. Her hair is undone, and it streams out. BERT *soaps it.*

BETTY: Make it lather up. Push all the thoughts, the bad thoughts, push them out of my head.

BERT: Push 'em out. Push 'em out.

BETTY, *loving the shampoo:* Wasn't he disgusting?

BERT: That man?

BETTY, *looking at the flowers he brought:* Durwood Peach.

BERT: If you married him, you'd be Betty Peach.

BETTY: I'll give him his money back tomorrow.

BERT: Here comes the hot water!

BETTY: I'll keep half the money. A consideration fee. For considering his proposal.

BERT: Keep all of it. I don't want him around.

BETTY: No, I'll keep half the money in payment for a tormented night's sleep. For tossing and turning and wondering whether or not I should run away with an insane Good Humor man. Ex-Good Humor man.

BERT: Our flavor of the week: Betty Peach! Betty Peach on a stick! Here comes the shampoo. Make the bubbles come up. Work out all the bad thoughts.

BETTY: I went to visit Mavis in Memorial Hospital. She was dying of everything. They had cut off her breasts and she had lots of radiation treatment and her hair had gone. And I came to visit her. She was down to about sixty pounds and she wouldn't die. And I said, "Mavis, is there anything I can do for you?" And she said, "Yes, there is this new book: "The Sensuous Woman." Bring it. Read it to me." And I went all that summer in Boston. Every day for visiting hours and read her from this dirty book on how to be sensuous and how to be attractive and how to have orgasms and how to . . . All summer she wouldn't die. All summer I read to her. I finished the book. Mavis said, "Begin it again." And I'd have to get very close to her to read to her because it was on the ward and the other patients did not want to hear this dirty stuff. And her gums were black and her breath smelled like sulfur and her hair was gone and I'm reading her how to attract a man and she's smiling and hanging on. I never went back after one day. I couldn't go back. Fall was coming. I hated life. I hated Mavis. I hated. Rub the hair. Wash it out. More hot water. More bubbles. More soap. Get it all out of my head all the bad into a bubble and fly it away and pop it. Get it out. BETTY *has torn all the petals and leaves off the flowers.*

BERT, *very moved, tender:* The next time my biology teacher rubs his bald head and says "Grass doesn't grow on busy streets," I'll say, "Yeah and it doesn't grow on rocks either." I'll say that. I kiss your hair, Momma.

BETTY: And I kiss Mavis and you and Raulito and your father and the Dope King of Providence, Rhode Island, and my sister Rosalie and life for bringing us a thousand dollars through the door and I kiss life and I kiss all the people I ever loved . . .

BERT: Me! Me! Most of all me!

BERT *pours water over her hair. The soap is washed out.* DUR-WOOD *appears in the room. He is breathless and excited.*

DURWOOD: Is something wrong with me? I have you here and say goodnight like some goon. What am I being so polite about? I'm no goon. Good manners make you a goon. I'm trying to learn to listen to myself. Listen to what I want. Not what people tell me I should want. You must think I'm a goon. Only a goon would drive thousands of miles to find the only woman he ever loved, find her, then leave her and go back alone to a room in the Dixie Hotel by himself.

BETTY, *moving away from him:* What did I do to make you feel all this?

DURWOOD: I remember riding by your house looking up at the porch, ringing the bells extra loud so you'd come down and buy ice cream from me. Your mother was sitting there rocking and your father reading a paper and you and your sister crouching on the green steps holding your skirts down around your ankles talking so hard to each other.

BETTY: They're all gone mostly.

BERT: You're gonna catch a cold. You got to dry the hair or the wet picks up dirt. Ma?

DURWOOD: You and your sister walked down the steps still talking so hard you didn't even pay any attention to me and you bought vanilla and walked back up the stairs and sat down and kept on talking.

BETTY: What in God's name could we have been talking about?

DURWOOD: I said I want in. One day I'm going to be on that porch with that girl.

BETTY: Her leaving home? Some Ava Gardner movie?

DURWOOD: I realize now I wanted the girl and not the porch. *He takes out snapshots.* You got to come back with me. This house will be yours. All this land.

BERT: Look at all the fences. Everything is outlined.

DURWOOD, *tearing up the photos:* But if I had to choose between

where I live and you, I'd rip up everything I own because
the only landscape worth looking at is the landscape of the
human body. I kiss your Blue Ridge Mountains of Virginia. I kiss your Missouri and Monongahela and Sus-
quehanna and Shenandoah and Rio Grande. I kiss the
confluence of all those rivers. I kiss your amber waves of
grain. I kiss your spacious skies, your rocket's red glare,
your land I love, your purple mountain'd majesty. But
most of all I kiss your head. I kiss the place where we
make our decisions. I kiss the place where we keep our
resolves. The place where we do our dreams. I kiss the
place behind the eyes where we store up secrets and knowledge to save us if we're caught in a corridor on a dark,
wintry evening. And you, with your mouth, kiss my head
because that's the place where I kept the pictures of you
all these years. Come home with me to the hotel.

BETTY: I will come with you.

DURWOOD *takes her aside:* But you can't take the kid.

BERT: What is he saying?

DURWOOD: I don't want you having any children except what
comes out of us.

BERT: What are you talking?

DURWOOD: A family's like a body. A perfect body. The man's
the head. The woman's the heart. The children are the
limbs. I don't want any limbs from any other bodies. No
transplants allowed. You hear me? Only out of us.

BERT: What are you saying?

BETTY, *taking him aside, quietly:* Let me go down there and
check out the landscape. I'll send for you in a few days. I
swear. ROSALIE *appears in the light at left.*

ROSALIE: So they went to South Carolina. The two of them.
They left the boy home.

CAPTAIN HOLAHAN *appears in the light at right.*

HOLAHAN: So she claims. So she claims. The fact remains the kid is dead.

BETTY *holds out the money.* BERT *takes it.*

CURTAIN

A C T   T W O

———

BERT *comes downstage and sings in a clear voice:*

> I used to believe
> When I was young
> I understood
> Every note that was sung.
> Voices of sparrows
> Voices of blue jays
> Voices of robins
> Voices of Eagles.
>
> When I was young
> I used to pretend
> Through all of my life
> I'd have a friend
> We'd climb the mountains
> We'd cross the deserts
> We'd sail the oceans
> We'd solve the mysteries.

When I was young
I used to believe
In some other life
I was an Inca
Maybe a Druid
More like Egyptian
Pyramid builder
Leader of millions.

I used to believe
When I was young
I understood
Every note that was sung . . .

Voices of Eagles . . .

*The lights go out on him, come up on the Interrogation Room
at the Police Station.*

HOLAHAN: We had trouble tracking you down. You left town.
Everybody thought you had taken the boy with you.

BETTY: I went away for a few days. He's a big kid. He's supposed to be able to take care of himself. Boy scouts go off.
Survivor camps where they go off, kids, for three months,
four, in mountains. Kids go in forests for weeks and
months and they come out men and parents are ap-
plauded.

HOLAHAN: Bleecker Street ain't exactly survival camp.

BETTY: He was supposed to stay with people in the building,
people were supposed to look after him.

HOLAHAN: A fourteen-year-old kid? Where's your head, lady?

BETTY: Here. This whole area above the neck. I just didn't

desert him. I left him with money. I left him with a thousand dollars.

HOLAHAN: You left your kid with a thousand dollars?

BETTY: My friend that I traveled with gave it to him. To me. I gave it to Bert.

HOLAHAN: Even with inflation, a thousand's a lot of money.

BETTY: What I'm saying to you is find the person stole the thousand dollars, you'll find who murdered Bert. Said it. I said murdered Bert. I promised myself everything would be all right if I never mentioned the word murdered. If I just never said the word, I'd be all right. If I never said the word, the person who—*did* it—

HOLAHAN: The murderer—

BETTY: Would be found.

HOLAHAN: Stop running away from the fact!

BETTY: I am not running away from the fact—

HOLAHAN: Of the murder—

BETTY: I just promised myself I wouldn't name the fact. Not ever. You made me say the word.

HOLAHAN: Can I make you say another word you're avoiding?

BETTY: Confess? Mister, I can say the word Confess all that I want because saying the word Confess is like saying the word desk. Chair. Necktie. Dirt. Room. You. I have nothing to confess.

HOLAHAN: Where is this millionaire now?

BETTY: It was only a thousand.

HOLAHAN: This thousandaire. Where is he right now?

BETTY: South Carolina.

HOLAHAN: That's where you went?

BETTY: Solomon Ferry. The Peach family. Durwood. His father's name. He was a junior.

The lights come down on him as HOLAHAN *dials the phone.*

ROSALIE *appears in the light at right. She drags a chair and she sits in it.*

ROSALIE: Scene. In which Betty wishes her sister was still alive so she could tell her what happened.

BETTY *sits against Rosalie's knees.* ROSALIE *listens with a compassion and intensity she'd never have out of a fantasy.*

BETTY: We got down to South Carolina two days after what a night at ye Olde Dixie Hotel. Durwood wasn't kidding all right. We came down this alley of trees and he says "Close your eyes and now turn 'em on." He had this farm with white fences. I never saw so many white fences. I'm not even talking about what went on inside the white fences. I'm a country girl. No stranger to green. The horses and cattle. I never saw such fences. And roads. White painted rocks lining the roads pointing the way where you go up to the big house. I said "Boy, old girl, you hit pay dirt this time. Boy, old girl," I said, "you have been on adventures in your short lifetime, but this is the key adventure. They're going to be doing TV spinoffs and shooting sequels to this part of your life. You are going to be a Southern lady." We stop in front of the white farmhouse and this youngish lady soon destined to be the ex-wife who wrote me the note struts out of the farmhouse followed by these two old people you just want to hug with a real nice parents' look followed by golden dogs the color gold of cough drops that rescue you in the middle of the night. Durwood gets out of the car and I let him walk around the car to let me out. And these people instead lead him in the house instead of letting him open my side of the door. The woman who would soon be Durwood's ex-

wife came back out and said "Are you the girl from
Maine?" I said "Yes, I was." She said "You're very kind
to bring Durwood back to us. Here's money." I got out of
the car. I said "I'm going to live here." The old people said
"Thank you for bringing our boy back to us. Here's
money. He had to get you out of his system. We let him
go to you. The doctors said let him go. It was the only
way." I said "Hey, this is going to be my house." "Well,
one thing, Durwood isn't crazy about," they said, "is you.
You sure are a pretty girl. He's been talking years about
you. But it's time he goes back in for a rest. There's a bus
leaving two oh five from Crossroads Corner going to
Wheeling, West Virginia, direct and you can make con-
nections there back to Maine." I said "New York. I live in
New York now." They said "Isn't that nice." They gave
me fifty dollars and showed me the hospital where Durwood would be which was very pretty too with a little
pond in the front of it and the dog rode in the car with us
and licked my face and I loved those old people and
asked them to take me with them. And they said "Here's
your bus," and I got on it.

The two sisters hold each other's hands. CAPTAIN HOLAHAN *puts
down the phone. The lights come up.* ROSALIE *goes into the
dark.*

HOLAHAN: We called the Peach family, honey.

BETTY: Don't call me honey. Okay?

HOLAHAN: They told us you were there.

BETTY: So I'm free. Alibis.

HOLAHAN: Honey, you don't need alibis for South Carolina.
    You need alibis for Bleecker Street. That's the required
    address of your alibis, honey. You could've killed Bert be-

fore you left so you wouldn't miss out on a joy ride to
southern climes. Your boy putting cramps deep in your life
style. The Peach family of Solomon Ferry don't tell me
nothing. The main event we're conferring about took
place in New York City.

*The piano plays melodramatically. The lights go out on Betty
and Holahan.* ROSALIE *appears by the piano. She speaks ur-
gently, like one of those action-news reporters covering a
live event. She remains onstage for the following scenes.*

ROSALIE: Scenes containing information the police would never
    know. Scenes containing information the mother would
    never know, never could know.

BERT *and* DONNY *appear.* BERT *is flashing some of Durwood's
money.*

BERT: Hey, Donny my man.
DONNY: Hey Mr. Bert my man.
BERT: Want to see what I got? Not so close.
DONNY: You want to sneak into Monosodium Glutamate?
BERT: What's your mouth talking, my man?
DONNY: M.S.G. That's what rock musicians call Madison
    Square Garden. Monosodium Glutamate. You know the
    stuff they put in Chinese restaurants that makes your face
    go all measles? You want to sneak in there tonight?
BERT: To a Chinese restaurant?
DONNY: To Madison Square Garden. They got hockey or a
    concert or a flower show.
BERT: My man, if I go to Monosodium Glutamate, I go walk-
    ing right in the front door paying my own way. *He takes
    out a bill.*

DONNY: Where'd you get a ten? You pulling jobs yourself?
Hey, I'm the man with the monkey. You into money now
by yourself? You deal me in. I got the dibs on the monkey.

BERT: No jobs by myself.

DONNY: You dealing? Coke? Pills? Is that more bills in there?
They counterfeit?

BERT: No, my man. They are real as a summer's day.

DONNY: Bullshit. Those are counterfeit. That's play money.

BERT: You want to see? We go into the bank.

The lights come up on a bank counter. THE TELLER *stands be-*
hind it. The music continues.

ROSALIE: They go into the bank on Sheridan Square. They wait
in line.

BERT, *to the teller:* My man, is this bill negotiable? What I'm
saying is there's no doubt about the accuracy of this de-
nominational piece of merchandise.

THE TELLER *takes the proffered bill and holds it up to the light.*

DONNY: They got a sign in the A & P saying beware ten-dollar
bills being circulated.

THE TELLER *smiles and hands the bill back.*

BERT: It's real? There's no doubts? And if I had more with
serial numbers right in line, they'd all be real too? Thank
you, my man. Here's a quarter. A tip for your appraisal.

ROSALIE: They walk away from the bank clerk. The bank is
crowded.

BERT *goes to a glass desk in the bank:* Come here. I want to do
something. It's a funny joke I saw about a bank. You

take—anybody looking?—a deposit slip and you write
on the back: Hand over all your money or I blow your
brains on the wall.

DONNY: Where'd you get that money?

BERT: Then you put the deposit slip back where it came from.

DONNY: Come on. Tell.

BERT: Then you wait.

RAULITO *enters the bank area. He takes a deposit slip, fills it
out, goes to the teller, who takes the deposit slip.* THE TELLER
*looks around panicky. He pushes a button. A siren. Gun
shots.* RAULITO *looks around, his chest covered with blood.
Blood comes out of his mouth.*

RAULITO: I come into the bank to make deposit number seventeen in the Christmas Club. Time to make deposit number
Seventeen. Christmas Club.

*He falls. His trench coat opens. His evening gown trembles
down. He falls against the counter. The lights go out. Music
up.*

DONNY: Buy me something. Your money's burning holes in my
pockets. Let's go.

ROSALIE: They go.

The stage is bare. JOANNE *has joined Bert and Donny. The
three of them walk in circles.*

DONNY, *to Joanne:* Hey, Joanne, Bert's crazy. You know what
he's doing? Putting razor blades in frisbees and then
when we see somebody we don't like from Elizabeth

Irwin High School, we toss it at them and say "Hey, grab!"

JOANNE: Papers I read a German shepherd ate a newborn baby.

BERT: Shut up, Joanne.

DONNY: Bert's mother's been gone two days now. She left him a lot of money.

JOANNE: The mother went out and left the baby for a moment and the dog ate the baby.

BERT: Shut up, Joanne. You're a real creep. My mother's right. You're a walking exorcism picture. All the time you're so creepy.

JOANNE: Your mother likes me.

BERT: She says you give her the creeps.

DONNY: Momma's boy.

BERT: I'm not!

JOANNE: You are so.

BERT: I like my mother being away. I got the apartment to myself. I'm eating good. Boy, my mother's a rotten cook. I see those commercials Food like mother used to make. I say Boy, that's the worst commercial God ever made.

JOANNE: Momma's boy.

BERT: Shut up. There's the restaurant where the bicycle got my aunt.

DONNY: What kind of bicycle?

BERT: Ten-speed Raleigh. Yellow.

JOANNE: You got the money. You could buy a ten-speed Raleigh yellow. If you weren't so chintzy.

BERT: No way. Money's got to last me.

DONNY: She was a nice lady.

BERT: That's how we came down to New York from Maine. We had her funeral, then we stayed and stayed. Wasn't for that ten-speed Raleigh whizzing around the corner, we'd still be in Maine.

JOANNE: Momma's boy.

DONNY: Where's your father? My mother says how come we never see Bert's father?

BERT: He's away on secret duty.

JOANNE: Oh sure.

BERT: He's on the payroll of foreign governments. He calls me all the time and asks me not to tell where he is because if it got out.

JOANNE: Oh sure.

DONNY: The CIA?

BERT: More secret than the CIA.

JOANNE: Nothing is more secret than the CIA.

BERT: If it's such a good secret then how come you know about the CIA. The place my father works for is so secret it don't have no name or initials or nothing.

JOANNE: Or existence. *She calls in the distance:* Hey, Margie? Want to sneak in to what's playing at the Greenwich? The Waverly? I don't care. *She goes.*

BERT: What a creep.

DONNY: German shepherds are gonna eat her some day.

BERT: Suppose one day your money runs out and you don't know anybody, what do you do?

DONNY: You work.

BERT: Fourteen you can't work. They put you in orphanages? You go to the police, they arrest you? What do you do?

DONNY: You got all this money.

BERT: Suppose it runs out.

DONNY: Thousand dollars don't run out.

BERT: Sure it can.

DONNY: You sure you got it?

BERT: You want to see it?

They run. Music plays. Threatening. Blackness. Then one spotlight shining down at center stage. They're in Bert's apartment.

BERT: Hello?
DONNY: You think there's anybody here?
BERT: Ma?
DONNY: Is she here?

BERT *runs in and out of the light.*

BERT: I hid the money behind the curtains. I hid the money in the toilet. I hid the money in the freezer. I hid the money under the bed. I hid the money in the oven. I hid the money under the carpet. I hid the money in the shower. I hid the money in our shoes. I hid the money in pockets of clothes we don't wear. I hid the money. *His arms are filled with the bills.* How long can it last me? Suppose somebody comes in the window? Suppose they steal the money? Who am I gonna call? It's not me. It's a friend. I'm talking about a friend. What if my friend gets locked out? How will he get back in? Is there an earthquake? Why is the room shaking? I can't stop shaking? Hold down the floor! I don't know where she is! She went away and left me! She went out the door! She left me! She went away! I'm turning to water! My stomach's coming up! The floor is moving! *He hugs Donny.*
DONNY *pauses:* Hey. Don't you hug me. Hey. You don't touch me. You hear me? You get your mitts off me. You hear.
BERT: I'm going away. Hang on to me.
DONNY: You keep your hands to yourself. You keep your hands. It was your idea bringing those guys up here and hitting them. You the one that brought them up. You

brought up too many. You got too many watches, Bert.
You stay away from me.

BERT: Suppose she never comes back?

DONNY *takes out his monkey wrench:* I know what this is. You
brought me up here to get my watches, didn't you. You
earned all that money. You brought me up here. You're
doing recruiting for those old guys down at the docks who
want kids.

BERT: Suppose she don't ever come back.

BERT *clutches Donny around his knees.* DONNY *lifts his monkey
wrench over Bert's head. They freeze.* ROSALIE *appears.*

ROSALIE: And all the dead people, the people who have died,
me, Raulito, Durwood, the Dope King of Providence,
Mavis Brennan, the man on the ten-speed bike, all the
dead people in our lives join together and lead Donny to
the wrench and put his hands around the wrench and lead
the wrench to Bert's head and we hold Bert's head so
Donny can bring the wrench down onto Bert's head with
greater ease. Bert falls. Donny takes the thousand dollars.
And at this time precisely, Betty was being put on a Greyhound bus at Crossroads Corner, South Carolina, and
being sent back to New York. Betty turns around in the
window and sees the parents of Durwood and Durwood's
wife waving goodbye.

JOANNE *runs into the apartment area. She knocks on the door.*

JOANNE: Bert? Donny?

DONNY: Go away.

JOANNE: You in there?

DONNY: Get out of here, Joanne.

JOANNE: I'm coming in.

DONNY: You stay outside there.

JOANNE: I just got a summer job.

DONNY: Don't come in.

JOANNE: Checkout girl at the A & P. JOANNE *is trying to push the door in.* DONNY *is trying to hold it shut.* JOANNE *pushes the door in.* DONNY *falls back.* You got to be very strong to be a checkout girl at the A & P.

DONNY: You tell and I'll.

JOANNE, *after walking around and around Bert:* That's what a dead person looks like?

DONNY: He made me do it.

JOANNE: All the time you read about dead people and hear about dead people but this is my first. Not embalmed or anything.

DONNY: He tried to touch me.

JOANNE: Just regular dead.

DONNY: He put his hands on me.

JOANNE: I'm glad it's Bert. I'd hate my first dead person to be a stranger.

DONNY: I'm not ever going to not believe in dreams again. I dreamed the other night and the night before that and once about six months ago that a yellow checker cab stopped and a man got out and dragged me in and when the cab stopped we were in a quiet warehouse so you could look down and see the river and waiting in a line was all these men with drool coming out of their mouths and my feet were in cement and the old man touched me only he wasn't old anymore and that dream came true just now. Bert was the old man. My feet were in cement. I am not going to end up my life in any dream. I stopped that dream. Anybody tells you dreams don't tell the future you send them to me. JOANNE *holds Donny.*

JOANNE: We'll say somebody killed him.

DONNY: Who killed him?

JOANNE: One of those guys you bring up here with the watches.

DONNY: I don't want any part of it. Cops up here. They'll find fingerprints.

JOANNE: Okay. They've had all those murders down at the docks. We'll put Bert in a bag and bring him down the river and leave him there. By the warehouse.

DONNY: But those murders. The school-crossing lady told me those bodies—they had no heads. The maniac takes the heads off.

JOANNE: You got a saw?

DONNY: There's one out there.

JOANNE: You start cutting. Put papers down.

DONNY: Is this a crime!

JOANNE: He's already dead. You're making a mess.

DONNY: My uncle saw a dirty movie and he told me Bert's mother was in it.

They take Bert by the feet and drag him into the dark.

JOANNE: Bert wasn't from here. Bert never belonged here.

They are gone. ROSALIE *steps forward.* BETTY *appears in the light, at a phone. She dials.*

ROSALIE: Betty is now in Washington, D.C. She roams around Washington, D.C., looking at monuments. She buys a dress to calm herself. She calls Bert at a pay phone.

The phone rings. The lights come up on the apartment. DONNY *and* JOANNE *come into the overhead light area.*

JOANNE: Don't get it.

DONNY: It might be for me.

JOANNE: Don't get it. I'll wait for you outside.

The lights go out on Donny and Joanne and Betty.

ROSALIE: Betty hangs up. She walks to the Capitol building to look for the Declaration of Independence she saw printed on parchment paper like the original. She will bring it home to Bert for a present.

The lights come up center stage to signify the street.

DONNY: I'm finished. I put him in a duffel bag.

The two of them drag the bag.

JOANNE: Here's a shopping cart.

DONNY: We can't steal that. The A & P arrests you.

JOANNE: I'm going to be working there this summer. Employees are allowed to use them.

They load Bert's body in the bag into the cart. They begin pushing.

DONNY: You can smell the river tonight.

MARGIE *comes up.*

MARGIE: Hi. Joanne, could I talk to you?

JOANNE: Go away, Margie.

MARGIE: I got to talk to you.

JOANNE: Later, Margie.

MARGIE: What's in there?

DONNY: Margie, I believe Joanne was talking to you.

MARGIE: I want to see what you're pushing.

JOANNE: My grandmother's dog died and we're going to bury it in the river.

MARGIE: Can I talk with you? I don't want to go home yet. My mother's watching television. My father's kicking ass in the living room. *The three of them walk.* I went to the Waverly. My girlfriend held open the exit door. They had this movie there. A French picture. Reading the bottom lines in English while they're all above talking French. This picture was all about children. And a little French baby in the picture falls out of the nine-story window and lands nine stories on the ground and all the grownups scared shitless and the baby—God, I screamed —lands on a bush and jumps up and says Baby fall boom boom. The audience cheered. And later on this French grownup says That's childhood. They're protected forever. In a magic circle. Bad things happen to grownups but children are magic. I think that's what it said. I had to read fast and I was crying. I don't ever want to grow up. I'm afraid of getting out of school. I hate what's happening to my body. It's like it's a sin. I keep going to confession and confessing that things are happening to my body and the priest says But that's growing up and I say I don't want to grow up. I mean, I want to grow up so I can leave home and get a job and make some money and get a record player and get married, but I want my body to stop doing what it's doing. What kind of dog was it?

DONNY: I don't like it down here.

JOANNE: Look at the yellow cabs. People pulling up. Going into those warehouses. People climbing into those trucks.

DONNY: It's like my dream.

The cart tips over. Bert's head rolls out. MARGIE *screams.*
DONNY *puts it back in the bag.* JOANNE *takes Margie's hands.*
She and Donny put Margie's hands in the bag.

JOANNE: You're part of this forever and ever. You're part of it.

MARGIE: I'm out taking a walk.

DONNY: Here's money. Don't tell.

JOANNE: Shut up, Donny.

MARGIE: Where'd you get that money?

JOANNE: Don't give it to her.

DONNY: She'll tell.

JOANNE: She won't.

MARGIE: I got to go home!

JOANNE: You are a part of this.

MARGIE: I never saw nothing. My brain is dead. You hear me?
I swear? My eyes are blind. I was never out. My ears don't
hear. My brain is dead. I'm just out taking a walk. My
brain don't register nothing. My eyes don't see. Forever.
I'm never seeing nothing. Please. I'll see you. Later.
School. I'll see you tomorrow. That's all.

DONNY *and* JOANNE *push the cart into the darkness. There is
a splash. Darkness.* ROSALIE *steps forward. The piano plays
"Hey, Stay a While," very bouncily, cheerily.* ROSALIE *does the
stripper's walk while talking to us in the audience.*

ROSALIE: So Betty returned to New York, called Raulito to
make sure her job was still safe with Honeymoon Holidays and to make a wonderful joke about her southern
adventure of the past few days and she smiled because
she would make it sound funny like a wonderful guest
on the Johnny Carson show. Some Cuban relative answered the phone and told her Raulito was dead, shot

while trying to hold up the Chase Manhattan Bank. Betty laughed till she realized a truth was being told. She ran home and found police waiting there and when they told her Bert was dead, her son was dead, for a moment got Bert and Raulito mixed up in her head. They both couldn't be dead. She had this picture that her apartment had become a branch of Chase Manhattan and that's what Raulito was holding up. They took her down to the morgue and she asked why her son was on two tables. One large and one small. She identified his body. She identified his head. The room was identical to the one she had identified her sister in two years ago and somehow that comforted her, that she had been here before. She did not know, Betty, nor would she ever know that two drawers over from her son's was Raulito's body. Betty was taken into custody. Betty was questioned for a long time. Betty was released. Months went by. A summer. Joanne and Donny were very nice to her for a while but kids get new friends and kids forget and Betty hardly ever saw Bert's friends anymore. She draws a circle on a map and sees an island thirty miles off the coast of Massachusetts is the furthest she can get away from New York, from the mainland, with the sixty-odd dollars she has in her account. She gives up the apartment. She takes the bus to Massachusetts. She steps onto the ferry. She looks at the houses of great families on the shore. She talks with a man of quintuplets born many years ago. Talk of family and children. The sea is autumn calm. Seagulls fly above.

The music stops. The stage is filled with light. We are on the deck of the boat as at the beginning. HOLAHAN *and* BETTY *appear at the ship's railing.* ROSALIE *goes into the black.*

HOLAHAN: You recognized me?

BETTY: Captain Marvin Holahan. Sixth Precinct Homicide.

HOLAHAN *pulls off his disguise:* What did you write in that note?

BETTY *throws sheets of small papers into the wind. They blow away. She pours bottles overboard.*

BETTY: A confession. A full confession. I wrote down everything that happened. And it's all gone. There it goes. There's your case.

HOLAHAN: I got bounced. From the force. About six days after our meeting. I took a lot out on you. I was on probation at the time of that interrogation. I had a lot of secret pressures on me. I thought if I nailed you, they'd overlook this minor nothing drug bribe extortion rap they pinned on me which if the truth be known everybody on the force is involved with in one way or another. But they were looking for a patsy. I loved the way you stood up to me. I wanted you to be the killer. If I stayed on the force I would've found your boy's killer.

BETTY: No matter. I got on the bus this morning and I started writing on little pieces of paper everything I ever knew. Everything that ever happened to me. Sentences. Places. People's names. Secrets. Things I wanted to be. I thought maybe out of all that I'd find the magic clue who killed my kid. I'd say I see.

HOLAHAN: I tried to do investigations on my own to find the killer for a present to you. But you can't investigate outside the force. You need that power. You need . . . that secret power the force offers.

BETTY: It bothered me at first not knowing who killed Bert.

But then I thought of all the things we don't know. All
the secrets in the world got put in a bottle and thrown in
the sea and maybe someday I'll be walking along a beach
and the bottle containing the message for me will wash
up. If I don't know the answer, it's out there and one day
maybe an incredible coincidence will occur and I'll know
all I need to know. Or the murderer will come forward.
Or I'll even forget once I had a secret. I'll remember I
had a boy like I'll remember I once had a mother and
once had a father and I'll try to keep piling the weight on
to the present, so I'll stay alive and won't slide back. If I
don't know, somebody knows. My life is a triumph of all
the things I don't know. I don't have to know everything.
I read Agatha Christies and throw them away when the
detective says "And the murderer is . . ." The mystery's
always greater than the solution. I was terrified to have a
kid. I said before I got pregnant I'll have a kid and the
eyes will end up on one side of the face and all the fingers
on one hand and all the toes on one foot and both ears
on one side of the head. And Bert was born and he was
perfect. And this is the only thing I know. There's got to
be some order in there. I'm moving to this new place and
it has big houses with classical columns and maybe I'll
find a job in one of them in a house owned by an old man
who has an art collection and I'll read up on classical
painters and maybe he'll ask me to marry him or maybe
I'll kill him and get him to sign the collection over to me
or maybe I'll love him and marry him. Or maybe I'll dis-
cover a secret inside me that will make the whole world
better. I'm not discounting nothing. Maybe I'll be trans-
planted into somebody great who knows the secret, my
secret, or maybe I'll never know and a tornado or a water

spout will whisk me up and I'll turn into rain and end
up in that sea.

HOLAHAN: All I know is I know more about you than anyone
I know. All those months doing dossiers on you. All disconnected. All disjointed. Still I know more about you.
We both have to begin again. Maybe together? I could
reveal myself to you slowly. That was not me who inter-
rogated you. That was my job talking. That was unseen
pressures talking to you. That was saving my skin talking
to you. I feel for you. All what you've been through. I
feel for you. I read stories people falling in love who
threw acid in each other's faces and they get out of prison
and they still love each other. I read stories people try to
kill each other and end up loving each other. Give me a
chance? I got severance pay? I got enough to get us
through a winter?

BETTY *looks at him. She turns.* ROSALIE *appears at left. The
piano plays "Voices of Eagles."*

ROSALIE: Last scene. In which Betty remembers the conversation she and I had so many years ago, the intensity of
it burned into the Good Humor man's head. Betty has
tried to remember since that day what Rosalie, what I
had told her. She remembers. She and I sat on a summer
afternoon on the green porch steps. Our mother over
there. Our father over there. We pulled our skirts over
our legs.

BETTY *and* ROSALIE *stand side by side as young girls.*

ROSALIE: Stop shaking. Don't let them see. *To their parents:*
It's nothing, Dad.

BETTY: It's like my stomach's going to come up all the time.

ROSALIE: You're all right.

BETTY: How am I going to get through my life?

ROSALIE: Would you let me explain? Our spirits—it's so simple
—float around in space and it all makes sense when you
realize the planet Earth has these fishing hooks on it.
What we call gravity is fishing hooks and all the nice
things in the world are baited on those hooks and our
spirits floating up there all loose and aimless spy those
baited hooks and we bite. And we are reeled down onto
this planet and we spend the rest of our stay on this
planet trying to free our mouths of that hook, fighting,
fighting.

BETTY: But what do you do?

ROSALIE: You travel alone because other people are only there
to remind you how much that hook hurts that we all bit
down on. Wait for that one day we can bite free and get
back out there in space where we belong, sail back over
water, over skies, into space, the hook finally out of our
mouths and we wander back out there in space spawning
to other planets never to return hurrah to earth and we'll
look back and can't even see these lives here anymore.
Only the taste of blood to remind us we ever existed. The
earth is small. We're gone. We're dead. We're safe.

BETTY: But momma says—

ROSALIE: Oh, momma says. Momma says. When are you
gonna think for yourself?

BETTY: How do you . . . How can I think for myself? ROSALIE
has no answer. Bells ring. Vanilla? You want vanilla? We
hear you, Durwood!

ROSALIE *runs off.* BETTY *looks at* HOLAHAN. *A long pause. She moves toward him.*

CURTAIN

>The greatest poverty is not to live
>In a physical world, to feel that one's desire
>Is too difficult to tell from despair.
>
>—Wallace Stevens, *Esthétique du Mal*

BOSOMS
AND
NEGLECT

FOR ADELE

CHARACTERS

Henny
Scooper
Deirdre

Bosoms and Neglect, directed by Mel Shapiro, was presented by Bernard Gersten and John Wulp in association with Marc Howard at the Longacre Theatre, in New York City, on May 3, 1979. An initial engagement at the Goodman Theatre, Chicago, Illinois (Gregory Mosher, artistic director), opened March 1, 1979.

CAST

HENNY	*Kate Reid*
SCOOPER	*Paul Rudd*
DEIRDRE	*Marian Mercer*

The scenery was by John Wulp. Costumes were by Willa Kim. The lighting was by Jennifer Tipton.

PROLOGUE

Henny's apartment in Queens.
Summer storm. Rain. Thunder.
HENNY *sings in a raucous voice a pop tune along the lines of*
"Caught Between Two Lovers." Her voice comes from behind
the window curtain.
SCOOPER *lets himself into the apartment. He is forty, fit, trim.*

SCOOPER: I found a doctor who'll make house calls. *He passes*
   through the room without taking off his soaking wet rain-
   coat and hat. The singing continues. Offstage: Talk about
   Mission Impossible. I'm sorry I'm late. He'll be here in
   about fifteen minutes.
HENNY, *behind the curtain:* Oh God. Oh God. Oh God.

SCOOPER *comes back into the room holding an empty washed*
mayonnaise jar. He pulls back the window curtain. HENNY
stands there, her fingers in her ears, still singing. She is old.
She is blind. Her spirit is strong.

SCOOPER: This house-call doctor wants you to fill up a jar so he can take it to the lab. I have to bring it up to the pharmacy on Eighty-second Street. So can you fill this up?

HENNY: I don't have to go.

SCOOPER: *Now* you don't have to go.

HENNY: I don't have any cystitis.

SCOOPER: Don't go screaming and crying and shaking so hard. He can't get a look at you if you're screaming and crying and shaking so hard. I told him it burns when you pee. I told him it's probably cystitis. Don't close your ears and hum. Listen to me. Valerie said it sounds like cystitis. It's a ladies' sickness. Valerie said if it burns when she pees, it sounds like cystitis to me. I told the doctor it was probably cystitis. That's what Valerie says.

HENNY: Valerie doesn't know nothing. My bladder fell out.

SCOOPER: This magic doctor says "What does this mean, her bladder fell out." I said "That's what she says, her bladder fell out."

HENNY: My bladder fell out.

SCOOPER: It burns when she pees.

HENNY: It burns when I pee.

SCOOPER *hands her the bottle:* He has an Italian accent so when he comes don't go running out because he's a foreigner. He's a real Latin Lover type is what he sounds like. Take the bottle! And don't go falling in love with him when you hear his Latin accent.

HENNY, *feeling the bottle:* You'd have to be a contortionist in a circus to fit on this. What's wrong with you?

SCOOPER: What's wrong with *me* who finds a doctor who makes house calls? You got a juice bottle?

HENNY: My bladder fell out. I can feel it. Give me your hand. Touch it. Oh God. You can feel it.

SCOOPER: I'm not the doctor. Don't go using me as the doctor.

I'm not going to touch you there. *He goes out of the room.*

HENNY: This doctor's going to lock me up when he sees me. When he sees this bladder.

SCOOPER, *offstage:* The doctor's not the enemy.

HENNY: How do you know? You never saw him before.

SCOOPER: Valerie found him.

HENNY: He's going to run out of here screaming when he sees me.

SCOOPER *comes back into the room:* Doctors don't run out on patients. Crazy patients do the running out so the doctors can't treat them, fix them. Fill this jar. *He puts down a quart-sized juice jar.*

HENNY: It's . . . it's not just my bladder.

SCOOPER *picks up a carton:* Why does an eighty-three-year-old woman have a giant box of Super Kotex? You're not having reverse change of life? Medical marvels. What is this Kotex doing here?

HENNY: I thought it would go away.

SCOOPER: What would go away?

HENNY: I prayed to Saint Jude and said Saint Jude Patron Saint of Lost Causes, Patron Saint of the Impossible, Patron Saint of the Damned, take this away from me.

SCOOPER: Take what away from you?

HENNY: It bleeds and bleeds and I put Kotex over it and stand in front of the window all night in the dark looking up waving a statue of Saint Jude over it so it'll dry by the morning. But it never dries. It never stops bleeding. I sent out for more Kotex. It never stops bleeding. You're hurting my arm!

SCOOPER: What never stops bleeding?

HENNY: I never would've told you about the other incident, except my insides are falling out and I can't pee and I told

you and I could cut my tongue out because it don't hurt
that much when I pee. I could live with it. It's not so bad.

SCOOPER: This other incident?

HENNY: It doesn't hurt. If I could see, I could see it was nothing. But I can't see so I make it up in my mind that it's
more than it is, you see.

SCOOPER: Where is this incident?

HENNY: It's not hide-and-seek, for Christ's sake. I haven't got it
hidden in the back of the stove. It's here. It's me. The incident is me.

SCOOPER: How long?

HENNY: Not long.

SCOOPER: Deal straight. How long?

HENNY: It started in a way I could notice the day you and
Valerie and Ted came out here.

SCOOPER: That was two years ago.

HENNY: It started that day.

SCOOPER: What started that day?

HENNY: The skin broke that day.

SCOOPER: Skin where?

HENNY: It's not important.

SCOOPER: What skin broke?

HENNY: I can deal with this. My Kotex and Saint Jude and I
are very happy. I don't have to pee. If I can just work it
so I don't have to pee, I'm all right.

Door chimes sound.

SCOOPER: He's here. The doctor is here.

HENNY: Send him away.

SCOOPER: We'll hold you down and strip you and find this incident.

HENNY: It feels better. Go away.

SCOOPER: What skin broke?

HENNY, *impatiently:* Oh God. Here. *She opens her blouse. He steps back.* It doesn't look so bad. Does it? Real false alarm. Girl who cried wolf. One day something will be wrong with me and you won't bother to help me because I dragged you out here once before for a little nothing. You're too young to have problems. I don't want to burden you with my problems. You want to send out to that new Italian deli for shrimp salad? They use real shrimp. None of those little plastic pinkies. I buy it to last two days and it's gone before I'm even ready for dinner.

SCOOPER: Oh dear God. Oh Christ. Jesus H fucking Christ.

HENNY: There is no reason for such language. Saint Jude does not like it. Want me to go to the door and tell the doctor to go away? False alarm time? I'll give him five dollars. See my system? The five-dollar bills have one safety pin in them. The tens I have the girl put two safety pins in. The ones are on their own. *The door chime sounds.* Tell him April Fool. Say Saint Jude helped a supposed lost cause make a miraculous recovery.

SCOOPER *goes off. She stands smiling, her blouse open in the light.*

SCOOPER: Doctor, you'd better get in here.

HENNY: No!

BLACKOUT

ACT ONE

———

Deirdre's apartment in the East Sixties. Lots of books. Two couches. Light streams in. A section of the room is used as an office, with Jiffy mailing envelopes, wrapping paper, twine, a stamp machine, and a scale.

DEIRDRE *is in her thirties. Very beautiful. Very intense. She holds a drink and leans forward listening to* SCOOPER. *He sits on the other couch. A packed suitcase is by the door. It is Scooper's.*

SCOOPER: Imagine a peach that had an enormous bite taken out of it.

DEIRDRE: Oh Christ.

SCOOPER: I'm not finished. Then. Then.

DEIRDRE: Calm.

SCOOPER: Was left in the back of a disconnected refrigerator for the winter months and you come back in the spring and open the ice-box door and find the peach rotted where the bite was taken out. This poison gauze. This penicillin rot-mold. You could put your fist into the hole in her breast. The cancer was that deep.

DEIRDRE: Wait.

SCOOPER: She stood there, her blouse off. It's not so bad, she keeps saying. It is not so bad.

DEIRDRE: It's impossible. What you're describing.

SCOOPER: I saw it.

DEIRDRE: Cancer works slowly.

SCOOPER: I am telling you—I can't believe you are not believing me. I pour this out and your response is ...

DEIRDRE: I'm not saying you're hallucinating. I'm saying cancer works inside, silently. Not like some horror show in a Drive-In.

SCOOPER: She had so neglected herself that the disease was sick of not being noticed. The disease finally burst through her skin. The ulceration was like this screaming flesh, this breast—screaming how loud do you have to go to get noticed?

DEIRDRE: Oh Christ.

SCOOPER: The good part about being that old the metabolism moves so slowly that the cancer takes just that much longer.

DEIRDRE: And she had no medical aid?

SCOOPER: Sure. For two years, she's been laying Kotex over the wound, waving this tan plastic statue of Saint Jude, Patron of Lost Causes, over this small, expanding cavity in her chest, standing all night in the dark privacy of her open window so the midnight air would dry it out.

DEIRDRE: You never noticed?

SCOOPER: I never saw her.

DEIRDRE: In two years?

SCOOPER: She only likes talking on the phone. I can't see her. She can't see me. Gives her equal footing.

DEIRDRE: But her bladder—

SCOOPER: It was her uterus.

DEIRDRE: Oh dear God.

SCOOPER: It fell out.

DEIRDRE: Oh no.

SCOOPER: Eighty-three-year-old muscles give out.

DEIRDRE: But still—

SCOOPER: The doctor who made the house call said this woman is finished. This woman will not make it through the day. It's not so bad. Girl who cried wolf. False alarm." I paid off the doctor. Got Doctor James on the phone. Got her up to Columbia-Presbyterian.

DEIRDRE: The best.

SCOOPER: Doctor James waiting right there. He had a bed waiting, the best surgeon all lined up to see her.

DEIRDRE: That was yesterday?

SCOOPER: That was yesterday.

DEIRDRE: And today she's on the table?

SCOOPER: Right now.

DEIRDRE: It makes *me* feel so well taken care of, like a great fringe benefit, if anything happened to me.

SCOOPER: Thanks to Doctor James.

DEIRDRE: A toast to you.

SCOOPER: To me?

DEIRDRE: To him.

She pours wine. White, chilled. Cool. They toast.

SCOOPER: After two years of lying and hiding.

DEIRDRE: You?

SCOOPER: Her. *They sip.*

DEIRDRE: Poor tragic lady. Outliving her friends. Standing all night at a window. Not trusting any human being enough to reach out.

SCOOPER: Don't forget the statue she's waving over her breast. Significant detail. Saint Jude. Patron of Lost Causes.

DEIRDRE: I suddenly have this image of being blind. Oh God. Never to be able to browse. I could never learn Braille. The skin on my fingers might be too tough to let the words come through.

SCOOPER: She elected to go blind.

DEIRDRE: You don't cast votes to be blind.

SCOOPER: Twenty years ago she did. She marched right up to the polling booth with her glaucoma and cataracts. Her hysteria rendered her untreatable. She looked at my father and me with these eyes turning to milk, the sight curdling out of them. "You're lying to me, it's something worse. Tell me the truth. No, don't tell me the truth. Lie to me." She begged us to lie to her. We said we *were* telling the truth. She said that's the biggest lie. And she invented some exotic disease for herself. And she proceeded to go bonkers and embark on a series of suicide attempts as if the "Guinness Book of Records" suddenly had an opening.

DEIRDRE: And she's still nuts?

SCOOPER: As soon as she went blind, her mind snapped back like the price of gold. She was still alive. Nothing worse had gone wrong with her. She believed the disaster. She was only blind. That she could live with. You become saner much quicker than you go mad. So we had ten years of suicide attempts. And now the last ten she's been feeling her way around like a lost company of *The Miracle Worker*.

DEIRDRE: Your father?

SCOOPER: He stroked out along the way. One day he just short-circuited while she was eating a light bulb . . . or a knife. Stop looking at me that way.

DEIRDRE: Do you find it so difficult taking care of another human being?

SCOOPER: She did it herself.

DEIRDRE: I see why you go to Doctor James.

SCOOPER: Sight is a collaborative act, requiring subject and object working together in trust and tranquillity. You have to tell the doctor what you're seeing and if you're screaming and have flames shooting out of your ears— *He downs his drink. He looks around at all her books.* Are you in publishing?

DEIRDRE: I buy and sell. From estates. First editions.

SCOOPER: You could have two lions in front of your door.

DEIRDRE: How old is she?

SCOOPER: Eighty-three.

DEIRDRE: Then why don't you let her die?

SCOOPER: Because I don't want that solution in me. She is not allowed to take that *out.* Hysteria is not an *out.* Fantasy and panic are not *outs.* I don't want the solution of suicide in my genes. I want courage in my genes. I want strength in my genes. I want seeing problems *through* in my genes. That old lady is going to stay alive and die of old age and plain old-fashioned wearing out. She is not going to be killed by an overactivity of the most valuable thing we have, our imagination. Look, you've got your own problems.

DEIRDRE: No! No! Really! I'm an ear. I love to be an ear.

SCOOPER: Still. He died right here? *He touches her hand.* It must have been a shock.

DEIRDRE: The air conditioner was off. I thought I'd suffocate and I couldn't open any windows, all sealed shut to keep the air conditioning *in*, and I turned on the lights and they flickered and went out and my transistor said it was three A.M. and a hundred degrees. I had this flashlight and picked up anything to read, just for the reading, just till it got light ... "Tess of the D'Urbervilles."

SCOOPER: Thomas Hardy!

DEIRDRE: And Raymond leaps up. His paws cover the text. I say "Down, Raymond!" And Raymond gasped with the lack of air and falls over. Right here. Tongue hanging out. I didn't know what to do. Please let it be light! Finally it got to be time and I put on this dress and ran out.

SCOOPER: And you come back and he's gone?

DEIRDRE: Wait. The air conditioner's on.

SCOOPER: Who'd break in and kidnap a dead dog?

DEIRDRE: I see! My husband! Of course.

SCOOPER: Your husband?

DEIRDRE: Came back. Saw what happened. Took Raymond up to the animal hospital for disposal. Or the ASPCA. I'm glad that's solved. And the air conditioner turned on. Oh dear, the idea of a thief who breaks in and takes only dead pets. That's even too strange for a city of strange tales. Raymond will be back soon and all questions will be solved.

SCOOPER: Raymond? Will be back?

DEIRDRE: My husband. *She resumes packing books in boxes.* I really have to get back to work. Charles Dickens off to Honolulu. *She packs books busily.*

SCOOPER: Your husband and your dog have the same name?

DEIRDRE: That should tell you all you need to know about my marriage.

SCOOPER: I'm sorry.

DEIRDRE: It's all over. Nothing. Really. Hand me John Updike.

SCOOPER, *bringing her the books:* He must be a great help.

DEIRDRE: John Updike?

SCOOPER: Doctor James.

DEIRDRE: I read somewhere once the reason people have to go

to doctors is the impossibility of the human being to say
goodbye.

SCOOPER *picks up some books:* Beautiful bindings. Uncut.

DEIRDRE: I specialize in uncut.

SCOOPER: The weight. The smell. The feel. *She takes the books
away from him.*

DEIRDRE: I was touched when you introduced yourself.

SCOOPER: You didn't say "Who is this asshole coming up to me
in a Fifth Avenue bookstore?"

DEIRDRE: You're hardly a stranger.

SCOOPER: I stumbled out in the street this morning. Have a
wonderful vacation, Doctor James. Don't dare ask him
where he's going. Ooops, didn't mean to ask. Should I
kiss him? Filial peck on the cheek? Yearly affection. Will
he think it's a pass? Decide against. Out in the street.
Jesus. Only Nine Fucking Forty Fucking Five A.M. How
am I going to get through this day?

DEIRDRE: Already eighty-eight degrees.

SCOOPER: I run to Doubleday's. Fifty-Seventh and Fifth. Wait
for it to open. Cool. See what new books have come in
since yesterday.

DEIRDRE: But it was like two degrees Celsius.

SCOOPER: Spy. Sex. Show Biz. Something to turn the page.

DEIRDRE: I cannot figure out Celsius.

SCOOPER: And what do I see when I get to the corner? You.
Looking in the bookstore window. Waiting for it to open.
Your dress swaying slightly. How did your legs find the
only breeze?

DEIRDRE: I mean, who *is* Celsius?

SCOOPER: You looked so healthy.

DEIRDRE: I *am* healthy.

SCOOPER: I didn't think you'd.

DEIRDRE: Of course I.

SCOOPER: But you moved away.

DEIRDRE: I didn't think you'd. After months of silence.

SCOOPER: I'd never seen you move. Only sit. The waiting room. Turning pages. Reading copies of *Vogue*.

DEIRDRE: Long gone out of vogue.

SCOOPER: I looked at you staring in the bookshop window and I said this woman and I share the deepest experience of a lifetime and we have never spoken a word. I have even come from a couch that was still warm from you.

DEIRDRE: You followed me.

SCOOPER: To Rizzoli's.

DEIRDRE: The foreign bookstore.

SCOOPER: Is that woman as paralyzed as I am about Doctor James going away for a month?

DEIRDRE: Thumbing through glossy foreign magazines, looking around to see if you were following me. I pick up *Oggi, Paris Match, L'Express*.

SCOOPER: I thought you'd be glad to hear an American voice.

DEIRDRE: Just because someone speaks the same language doesn't mean you can trust them.

SCOOPER: You recognized me.

DEIRDRE: I recognized you.

SCOOPER: "Would you like to have a drink?"

DEIRDRE: "My dog's died and it's eighty-eight degrees and it's just ten A.M. and I don't know what to do."

SCOOPER: "I could help you."

DEIRDRE: "I live around the corner."

SCOOPER: "Around the corner." My God, across the street from Doctor James. I didn't think real people lived on this street. All the Mercedes lined up to haul our pains away. I thought you had to be a shrink to live here.

DEIRDRE: A friend of mine calls this street the Mental Block.

SCOOPER: A close friend?

DEIRDRE, *avoiding the question:* Actually I read it.

SCOOPER: Who's with him now?

DEIRDRE: The mother who drinks.

SCOOPER: Oh Jesus. She once came out of the office and asked me for drink money right in the waiting room.

DEIRDRE: She did the same to me!

SCOOPER: I felt so guilty refusing her.

DEIRDRE: I had to have my session switched.

SCOOPER: Look! There she is!

DEIRDRE: Stand back!

SCOOPER: She's walking so straight.

DEIRDRE, *watching her go:* Sober.

SCOOPER: Healed.

DEIRDRE: A cab pulls up. Out gets the pianist. He runs in, late for his appointment.

SCOOPER: He didn't play for years. That poor genius. Too crazy to play.

DEIRDRE: I have his new record.

SCOOPER: I went to his concert.

DEIRDRE: I was there!

SCOOPER: I thought: Doctor James healed this man so he can play again.

DEIRDRE *puts on a recording. Brilliant Chopin fills the room.*

DEIRDRE: I felt the same thing.

SCOOPER: It's like we're all related.

DEIRDRE: Brothers and sisters sent in for a private loving audience with our father.

SCOOPER, *calling:* We love you, Doctor James!!!!

DEIRDRE: This is no spy turret!

She turns off the music abruptly. SCOOPER *comes away from
the window and pours another drink.*

SCOOPER: You must know so much about him.

DEIRDRE: I know he's got a wife.

SCOOPER: Oh, I knew that.

DEIRDRE: Poor Doctor James.

SCOOPER: Poor?

DEIRDRE: That tragic marriage.

SCOOPER: Did he tell you he had a tragic marriage?

DEIRDRE: How could he understand my pain if he didn't have
his own? I hear it. There in his voice. That tormented
way his fingers rub that birthmark on his hand. Talk
about Rorschach tests. I never thought I had any imagination at all until I saw Doctor James's wine-colored
birthmark . . . like a magic token transforming me into
whatever I want to be. Clouds. Scudding by in the birthmark.

SCOOPER: What birthmark?

DEIRDRE: On his hand.

SCOOPER: Which hand?

DEIRDRE: I lie like this. Look over like this. Yes, the left hand.

SCOOPER: I never noticed any birthmark.

DEIRDRE: Did you notice FDR was in a wheelchair?

SCOOPER: Are you calling Doctor James a cripple?

DEIRDRE: It's the most obvious thing about him.

SCOOPER: You see a spot from luncheon. And you romanticize
the coagulation into a birthmark.

DEIRDRE: I have seen that birthmark every day for the past—
number of years and it is impossible to spill that much
gravy in the selfsame spot for the past—*number* of years.
Let's not make this one of those events like the song in

Gigi—"I Remember It Well"—based on Colette, where we talk about the same thing and have completely different perceptions of it. You have your Doctor James.

SCOOPER: I have *my* Doctor James.

DEIRDRE: I have my birthmarks. You keep of him whatever you want.

SCOOPER: All I ever see of Doctor James are his wing-tip shoes. I love the guy, but I hate his wing-tip shoes. They're like shoes that belong to some CIA agent.

DEIRDRE: How can you see his wing-tips?

SCOOPER: He crosses his legs. I quick turn up off the couch and look down and see the tips of his shoes.

DEIRDRE: Hating the wings at the tips of his shoes. So fascinating. Hating the fact that Doctor James can fly.

SCOOPER: Do you hear us romanticizing our doctor? We will have to tell him next September. He will laugh.

DEIRDRE: You think?

SCOOPER: You have to take risks.

DEIRDRE: I can never forgive them for taking the month of August off.

SCOOPER: They only do it so we won't run off to other doctors while they're away.

DEIRDRE: As if we'd go to anyone else.

SCOOPER: Sometimes I'll look at a friend in trouble and say Boy, if I trusted you more. Boy, do I have a doctor for you. Boy, could he tie those loose ends up in a minute.

DEIRDRE: But you don't.

SCOOPER: He's my secret weapon.

DEIRDRE: That's not being selfish.

SCOOPER: That's being protective.

DEIRDRE: I think you'd better go.

SCOOPER: Have I said—

DEIRDRE: It might not be healthy talking about our doctor this
way.

SCOOPER: I think he'd be thrilled. I can't wait to tell him.

DEIRDRE: You wouldn't dare tell him!

SCOOPER: To bring Doctor James a new character in my life
that he knows so well? You have to tell him about me.
You'll bring him me. I'll bring him you. To play his version of you against my version of you. To play your me
against his me. It'll be like "The Alexandria Quartet." The
air carbonated with all these realities and people! Poor
Lawrence Durrell. He's become so neglected.

DEIRDRE: Am I a major character or a minor character?

SCOOPER: Friends are always major characters.

DEIRDRE: Friendships are major responsibilities.

SCOOPER: I'm a wonderful friend.

DEIRDRE: Are you a five A.M. friend?

SCOOPER: A five A.M. friend?

DEIRDRE: A friend you can call and say stay on the phone till it
gets light.

SCOOPER: I read a book.

DEIRDRE: Sometimes a book doesn't help.

SCOOPER: You need a voice. I am a five A.M. friend.

They look at each other.

DEIRDRE: I . . . liked hearing about your mother. Father. Thank
you for trusting me with that.

SCOOPER: You don't have any family?

DEIRDRE: They were killed when I was very young.

SCOOPER: Oh dear.

DEIRDRE: Car crash home from skiing.

SCOOPER: Stowe?

DEIRDRE: Lake Placid.

SCOOPER: Never been to Lake Placid.

DEIRDRE: I went there once.

SCOOPER: I go to Stowe.

DEIRDRE: I have this golden photo of my parents. *She picks up a picture in a frame.* You can see the wit in their eyes. I've learned more about life staring at this picture taken shortly before their deaths trying to riddle out their smiles. Trying to find some injunction in their wrinkled noses. At one point in my life the picture seemed spiritual. I was going to school at a convent. I became a nun for a while.

SCOOPER: You were a nun?

DEIRDRE: I mistook gratitude for a vocation.

SCOOPER: I can't imagine you as a nun.

DEIRDRE: Believe me.

SCOOPER: I'd love to see that picture.

DEIRDRE: I show it to no one. *She puts it away in a drawer.* Doctor James says I read so much to make up their voices reading to me. I hear what I imagine their voices to be telling me about their lives. I read only the finest works. Their voices are very golden in my ear.

SCOOPER: You must be some patient for Doctor James.

DEIRDRE: When you said you'd come from the couch warm with me, you were saying you're in analysis. You don't sit up. I mean, you're not in therapy.

SCOOPER: I'm in analysis.

DEIRDRE: I couldn't talk to you if you were just in therapy.

SCOOPER: You can talk to me.

DEIRDRE: It's so snobbish but I wouldn't have respect for you if you were in therapy— I wish you'd get away from the window. I don't want him looking up and—

SCOOPER: Remember that fat girl—did you ever get a look at

her? She must've weighed in at a good four hundred pounds. I used to follow her at one time and I thought the couch would cave in—

DEIRDRE: "Ivanhoe" is an amazing book. It speaks with such an urgent clarity to today. Who'd think Sir Walter Scott would achieve—

SCOOPER: Oh my God, that wasn't you . . . was it?

DEIRDRE: Good God, I don't even know who you're talking about. Is that your idea of why people go to Doctor James? He's hardly a fat farm.

SCOOPER: It's just this girl—

DEIRDRE: Why did you go to Doctor James? Weight?

SCOOPER: One little problem that needed tying up.

DEIRDRE: One little problem? No such animal.

SCOOPER: I don't want to tell you anything that'll change your impression of me—

DEIRDRE: Luckily I have no impression of you at all. *She uncorks a wine bottle.*

SCOOPER: I think you're right. *He starts to go.*

DEIRDRE: You were saying why you went—

SCOOPER: He might be angry if he knew we were—

DEIRDRE: Try lying down on the couch—

SCOOPER: I don't want to tell you—

DEIRDRE: It might make it easier.

SCOOPER: He's not lucky enough to get orphans and nuns and husbands and dogs with the same name from me.

DEIRDRE: You're afraid you're not complicated enough? How silly! It's not a competition. How often do we get to share this magic part of our lives?

SCOOPER: It is almost religious with him.

DEIRDRE: Pater Noster. You and I. Brothers. Sisters.

SCOOPER: I'm an only child.

DEIRDRE: Family. That's what we are. We share family secrets.

SCOOPER: I started going to Doctor James because—ahhh. Sherlock Holmes. Beautiful edition . . . *She takes the book from him.* I started going to him because I was so happy.

DEIRDRE: So happy?

SCOOPER: I could live with my mother's suicide attempts and father's strokes. That was like wartime. That was easy. But for one period I stumbled inadvertently into some kind of happiness. Everything was strangely productive and rewarding and simple. I beamed out in this seraphic five A.M. joy why is everything so wonderful? And the Lispenards—*my* five A.M. friends—got me Doctor James's number to find out in a few quick sessions how this wanderer had stumbled into Shangri-La and how he could stay there.

DEIRDRE: And that was—

SCOOPER: Six years ago.

DEIRDRE: Are you still happy?

SCOOPER: Well, one thing led to another. And also Val.

DEIRDRE: Valium?

SCOOPER: Valerie.

DEIRDRE: Valerie?

SCOOPER: My old lady.

DEIRDRE: You don't mean your mother.

SCOOPER: My lady. My girl. My mistress. My blood. My brain. My heart. My wonder.

DEIRDRE: How nice of her to stand by you today.

SCOOPER: No, she's up in New Hampshire putting her kids in camp. Three of them. God, I'll be a father.

DEIRDRE: They're not by you.

SCOOPER: That's a whole other saga. She had Bradley and Kim and Sophie by Caesarean so she is still tight like a young girl and you come into her so firm and then suddenly it's like coming into St. Peter's in Rome, the way you round a small corner and the entire basilica is wide open in front of you. We have a good time in bed. She'll moan. I'll say "Darling, is that passion?" She says "No, for Christ's sake, I got this Joseph Conrad stuck in my ribs." We both have to have books in our pockets at all times. In our beds. On our walls. *He takes a paperback from his right jacket pocket.* Right now I'm traveling with Rilke. "Duino Elegies." Best poems written this century. *He takes a paperback from the left jacket pocket.* P. G. Wodehouse. "Luck of the Bodkins."

DEIRDRE: Hardly neglected.

SCOOPER: All the time I have to have a book. Words on the eyeball . . . it must create an erotic pressure. The physical rubbing of the words against the eyeball, kneading, prodding, massaging, grazing like this sensuous cow on the green pastures of your eye. And the thought, the illumination, the comprehension! Yes, that's the orgasm. You'd love her.

DEIRDRE: I must meet her.

SCOOPER: I even think of Doctor James as a literary experience. Before Doctor James, my life was pages spilled all over the floor. Grim. Violent. Aimless. He's edited my life into a novel I am so proud to be a part of. Jane Austen. That kind of clarity and effervescence. And intelligence.

DEIRDRE: Nothing's worth it if it's not a great artistic event.

SCOOPER: She wouldn't continue with me unless I kept up the therapy. I started doing the therapy as a bouquet for her. Then the therapy turned into analysis and here we are.

DEIRDRE: She sounds very positive.

SCOOPER: She is so healthy. She's been going to the shrink since she was about two. She has grown up on the couch. Then our affair sent her back into therapy.

DEIRDRE: Not Doctor James.

SCOOPER: No! She goes to group.

DEIRDRE: Group. Eccch.

SCOOPER: And her husband is in another.

DEIRDRE: She's married.

SCOOPER: The Loch Ness Monster lives.

DEIRDRE: Oh dear. Of course. The three children. St. Peter's Basilica.

SCOOPER: She was so unhappy over our affair and guilty that her husband began to feel guilty because he didn't know about our affair and started blaming himself for her grief, so he went into therapy and he was in one group and asked her join him in his group but she was already in another group and she wanted me to join the group her husband was in and then she'd join too, and I said I did not think that was a good idea.

DEIRDRE: I'm with you all the way there.

SCOOPER: I said I'll go to Doctor James for you, but no group analysis.

DEIRDRE: Only teaches you another kind of social chitchat.

SCOOPER: Unless it helps.

DEIRDRE: Of course. And what do your five A.M. friends say to all this?

SCOOPER: The Lispenards? It *is* the Lispenards. Valerie is one half of the Lispenards.

DEIRDRE: And the other half is—

SCOOPER: Ted. My college friend. My business partner. I suddenly see something so clearly. I get in a panic and I can't think straight. You have cleared my head. My God. I see. That vicious rotten human being. Literally rotten.

DEIRDRE: Valerie?

SCOOPER: My mother. She did it on purpose. She knew I was leaving. That's why she waited till yesterday. This operation. This cancer caper. All designed to keep me from

going. I don't know how she knew but she knew. Mystic
connection.

DEIRDRE: Don't assign her magic powers.

SCOOPER: You don't think she died.

DEIRDRE: On the table?

SCOOPER: Eighty-three. Wouldn't be unheard of. Oh Christ.

DEIRDRE: Believe it or not, mastectomy is simple surgery.

SCOOPER: May I use your phone? *He begins dialing.*

DEIRDRE: The breast doesn't involve any major body function
like breathing or digesting.

SCOOPER *speaks into the phone:* I'm trying to get information
on the outcome of an operation? Could you connect me
with— *To Deirdre:* They put me on hold.

DEIRDRE: She'll be all right.

SCOOPER: That breast nursed me. Fed me. My first connection.
All the time I spend pursuing wombs, hidden under in-
finities of skirts, entry to that warm darkness, and to see
what I'm searching for, hanging there. Light shining on
what no light should ever shine. This fucking old lady
thinks it's her bladder. If I'm conceived out of a bladder,
what does that make me? Get me off hold! Operator!
Operator! *He snaps the wine glass in his hand.* Godammit!!! DEIRDRE *runs out of the room.* I want the recovery
room! Okay. Back on hold. If that's the way you want it.

DEIRDRE *returns with a basin of water and bandages. She takes
his bleeding hand and washes it.*

DEIRDRE: "All happy families are alike." I don't know about
you but I always find Tolstoi very comforting.

SCOOPER: Are you a nurse?

DEIRDRE: I hope you're not a concert pianist. Don't have to
give a concert tonight.

SCOOPER: I'm an analyst.

DEIRDRE: But Doctor James—

SCOOPER: A computer analyst. Don't laugh.

DEIRDRE: I just had this mental image of all these angst-ridden computers jumping up on your couch. Help me! Help me!

SCOOPER: I love the way the light streams in your apartment.

DEIRDRE: I said once before I died I'd finally live in a place filled with light.

SCOOPER: Heat banging its fists against the window trying to get in. *Into the phone.* Operator! I'm here! Don't go away! *But she has.* Should I dial again?

DEIRDRE: Hang on there.

SCOOPER: O.K. Oh God. *He buries his face in his hands. Pause.*

DEIRDRE: You know who's tragically neglected? The Japanese. Kawabata.

SCOOPER: Is he the one with the private army who disemboweled himself?

DEIRDRE: That's Mishima.

SCOOPER: Is Kawabata the one who has the Japanese married couple traveling to all the puppet shows in Japan? A dying art to mirror a dying marriage?

DEIRDRE: No, that's Tanazaki.

SCOOPER: Is Kawabata the one who writes about the whorehouse where an old man rents drugged young girls and holds them in his arms all night, never fucking them. Just holding them.

DEIRDRE: That's Kawabata.

SCOOPER: So *that's* Kawabata. So neglected.

DEIRDRE: He won the Nobel Prize.

SCOOPER, *disdainful:* Pearl Buck won the Nobel Prize. What did you think about Isaac Bashevis Singer winning the Nobel Prize?

DEIRDRE: I cut something out of *TV Guide*. "Dick Cavett Show. Dick's guest tonight will be the singer, Isaac Bashevis."

SCOOPER: You have to show that to me.

DEIRDRE: I showed it to Saul Bellow and he was sending it out for Christmas cards.

SCOOPER: You know Saul Bellow ? ? ? ? ?

DEIRDRE: Well . . .

SCOOPER: You know someone who won the Nobel Prize ? ? ? ? ?

DEIRDRE: Oh, he's not my only Nobel Prize winner. I cradled Samuel Beckett in my arms right over there. Norman Mailer passed out there. I have authors in and out of here.

SCOOPER, *into the phone*: Yes? I'm calling to see if my mother has come down from surgery yet? I know you're busy but —her name is—has she even gone into surgery? I'm not trying to sell this info to the Chinese, believe me. You advise me not to stay at the hospital while the operation's on but then you won't—she's blind, she'll wake up and not know where—there was a brownout?

DEIRDRE: Happened here this morning. Lights just dim.

SCOOPER: Nobody's gone into surgery yet? When are they going into surgery? I have a plane to catch! *He slams the phone down*. She hasn't even gone in yet.

DEIRDRE: Leaving?

SCOOPER: Five o'clock.

DEIRDRE: Tonight?

SCOOPER: Haiti.

DEIRDRE: This time of year?

SCOOPER: She's trying to stop me.

DEIRDRE: The sidewalks are buckling and you're going to the jungle?

SCOOPER: It's so blindingly clear.

DEIRDRE: Don't people usually go to Haiti in the winter?

SCOOPER: She's been saving that breast to whip out just at an instant like this.

DEIRDRE: The heat in August. Frying pan. Fire.

SCOOPER: Hiding that whammy there in her bra.

DEIRDRE: But I suppose it's a different kind of heat.

SCOOPER: To stop me with guilt. Stop me with caring.

DEIRDRE: But people *always* say a different kind of heat.

SCOOPER: The caring is over.

DEIRDRE: Still hot is hot.

SCOOPER: My heart is sealed up.

DEIRDRE: On the other hand—

SCOOPER: I have to keep reminding myself she is a crazy old lady crippled by fear. Two years at a window waving plastic statues of fictional saints over a bleeding breast. God, Haiti. Tropic. Lush. She's not stopping me. Olaffson's Hotel. Great white Victorian bric-a-brac gingerbread hotel there in the jungle. Victorian. Voodoo. Volcanoes.

DEIRDRE: If you need any Valium.

SCOOPER: I'll have Valerie.

DEIRDRE: You're taking Valerie?

SCOOPER: Our first trip together. Finally. The decision.

DEIRDRE: What does her husband say to all this?

SCOOPER: We haven't told him yet. We've left a letter for him at his group tonight. We felt that was the kindest thing to do. He goes right from work to group. He couldn't read a letter like the one we've left him alone. He's so dependent on his group. Poor weak . . . don't get me started on Ted.

DEIRDRE: Should be an interesting session.

SCOOPER: In a way I'd like to be there. What was Hemingway's phrase? Grace under pressure? I don't think Ted Lispenard will personify grace under pressure.

DEIRDRE: And you'll be in Haiti.

SCOOPER: Four weeks.

DEIRDRE: The time Doctor James is away.

SCOOPER: Her sister will take the kids. When we get back we'll start looking for a place in Maine. Get out of this neurotic city. Find a beat-up ramshackle house by the sea. Remodel it. Books. Music. Comfort. Valerie says she wants a house like us. Simple on the outside. But inside. Inside! We have this dream of buying up every book in Maine.

DEIRDRE: That shouldn't be hard.

SCOOPER: Open the world's greatest bookstore. Get out of computers and machinery. Publish newsletters written by people telling what books they love. A bookstore open twenty-four hours a day.

DEIRDRE: Like L. L. Bean.

SCOOPER: Yes! People will flock to us from all over the world and we'll grow and grow until one day the entire town is one bookstore.

DEIRDRE: The elephant graveyard.

SCOOPER: A Vatican of books. "If we don't have it, they didn't write it."

DEIRDRE: You'll finish your treatment?

SCOOPER: Finishing my treatment is not the most important thing in the world. I'm almost finished with Doctor James anyway. Except for this one dream I have that even the great dream-decipherer himself can't figure out.

DEIRDRE: Please? I might be able to help—

SCOOPER: I am this little boy. All dressed up.

DEIRDRE: New clothes. Masquerade.

SCOOPER: A strange city.

DEIRDRE: Outsider. Go on.

SCOOPER: Facing a strange man.

DEIRDRE: And you're a small child. And it's not your father. Hmmm.

SCOOPER: And my mother who is all dolled up—

DEIRDRE: A new beginning?

SCOOPER: Picks me up and begins hitting this man with me.

DEIRDRE: Using you as a weapon?

SCOOPER: And she's screaming You neglected me! You neglected me!

DEIRDRE: And then you wake up?

SCOOPER: It's so alive in my mind.

DEIRDRE: I could figure that out.

SCOOPER: I really wish you wouldn't.

DEIRDRE: Strange city. Outsider. A dream of betrayal.

SCOOPER: I didn't say betrayal. I said neglect.

DEIRDRE: Neglect is always betrayal.

SCOOPER: Is that a quote?

DEIRDRE: That's a belief.

SCOOPER: If he can't figure it out—talk about "Pride and Prejudice"—I don't think you can. Stay out of it. O.K.?

DEIRDRE: I'll butt out of your head. Fine.

SCOOPER: But I know the key to everything is in that dream.

DEIRDRE: Oh, I see! If you solve the dream, you'll have to leave him.

SCOOPER: I want to leave him!

DEIRDRE: I didn't say you didn't.

SCOOPER: He's getting a postcard from me with a volcano on it and the message reads Doctor, see this volcano? This is me . . . Suppose she's dead. Suppose she died?

He picks up the phone and dials: Columbia-Presbyterian—is this? What number have I? *He puts the phone down in agony, then gets his face into a big smile. He lifts the phone again.*

Ted. Hi! What are you doing home? No, my fingers
were just dialing. And I dialed. Summer cold? Oh no.
They're the worst. Go back to sleep. You shouldn't answer
the phone if you're sick. Are you going to group tonight?
No, you mustn't miss that. Take care. Oh. Valerie called?
What time did she leave for New Hampshire? Great.
Listen, thank you for the flowers. She was barely in the
hospital when the flowers arrived. Really sweet. I don't
know yet. But the best doctors. Could you do me a favor?
Valerie wanted a report on how my mother is. I'm not at
home. Could you give her the number where I'll be.
680-3779. I'll be here. A friend. I'll call later. *He hangs
up. He is furious.* Asshole. You don't send flowers to a
blind person. You treat her senses. You send candy. That's
Ted in a nutshell. Oh, fuck. This atmosphere of lying.
Everyday for the past five years, living life with this Pav-
lovian smile trapped on my face. Inside I'm dying. A
Madame Tussaud's perfect wax smile.

DEIRDRE *turns away from him. She looks back at him with
disdain.*

DEIRDRE: Betraying your five A.M. friends.
SCOOPER: It didn't seem like betraying. The love sweetened
    everything.
DEIRDRE: You mean it poisoned everything. Like the silence of
    your mother's sickness.
SCOOPER, *reaching for a book:* Joseph Conrad. "Chance"! This
    is one of the books stuck in Valerie's ribs.
DEIRDRE, *disillusioned:* One of the great neglected master-
    pieces.
SCOOPER: I love this damned book.

DEIRDRE: So did I.

SCOOPER: "Life demands a man and a woman." *He searches through the book.*

DEIRDRE: Page 432. "Pairing off is the fate of mankind."

SCOOPER, *reading:* "If two beings thrown together, mutually attract . . . voluntarily stop short of the—the *embrace*—"

DEIRDRE, *quoting:* "they are committing a sin against life. The call of which is simple."

BOTH: "Perhaps sacred."

A pause. They look at each other.

SCOOPER: It's taken Valerie and me five years to get to this day. I don't want to get mixed up with another married lady.

DEIRDRE: I'm not married.

SCOOPER: Raymond.

DEIRDRE: There is no Raymond. I only told you that—a girl has to be—a woman has to be—I call myself a woman when I'm working, but when I'm alone in this apartment, I'm a girl. A girl has to be careful. I don't know you. A patient. I don't know what you're seeing him for. You might be a psychopath. I wanted you to think someone was coming home.

SCOOPER: You wear a wedding ring.

DEIRDRE: A friend advised me to. It avoids hassles.

SCOOPER: A close friend?

DEIRDRE: What time is your plane?

SCOOPER: Five o'clock.

DEIRDRE: Busy day. Very active. Very healthy. Haiti. "Comedians."

SCOOPER: I don't know who's playing down there.

DEIRDRE: Graham Greene. Novel. Haiti. In this pile.

SCOOPER: I've never read that.

DEIRDRE: I'd like to give it to you.

SCOOPER: Sign it?

DEIRDRE, *digging angrily in the stacks:* Where the fuck is it? Here. In the Evelyn Waugh pile. That's neglected. When one author ends up in another author's pile.

SCOOPER: They're all English. Easy mistake.

DEIRDRE: Your hand is all right?

SCOOPER: All fine.

DEIRDRE, *writing in the book:* "Be careful in the jungle."

SCOOPER: You sound like my mother.

DEIRDRE: Why did you pick me up today?

SCOOPER: I told you. The breeze around your legs—

DEIRDRE: We shared the same waiting room for so many months in silence. I spend so many sessions asking Doctor James, Why isn't that man looking at me? I even got it into my head that Doctor James had hired you to drive me mad, to ignore me, to come for your session even before my session.

SCOOPER: I came to prepare. To calm myself. A quiet place to read.

DEIRDRE: You'd loom outside that door. I'd be inside on the couch. You'd be out there, doing God knows what. Listening at the door. Laughing at me.

SCOOPER: Never. I was reading.

DEIRDRE: I begged Doctor James to change appointments. Please! I don't want to be annihilated by that man.

SCOOPER: And he only said Why does the presence of that man annoy you?

DEIRDRE: You *were* listening.

SCOOPER: How could I hear with his air conditioner on?

DEIRDRE: You became my father. My lovers. My teachers. My uncles. My bosses. Every man who's ever gone out of his way to ignore me. I found myself dressing for you. Would he notice this? I'll show him. I would stand up naked in this window and wait for you to come out of your appointment. I'd do hypnotism things. Now he'll look up. Now he'll see me.

SCOOPER: I was deep in my own problems.

DEIRDRE: So you missed my breakdown.

SCOOPER: When was it?

DEIRDRE: Last October.

SCOOPER: Last October. That was a rough time for me last October.

DEIRDRE: I had one of the world's greatest uninstitutionalized breakdowns with weeping and moaning and Doctor James pulling magic tricks out of the air to keep me out of a hospital and you sit there turning the pages.

SCOOPER: I was reading Herman Melville.

DEIRDRE: You ignore me for eleven months and today you are suddenly obsessed with unculminated desire to pick me up.

SCOOPER: You're an attractive woman.

DEIRDRE: I have been for the last eleven months. It's still the same flesh.

SCOOPER: Edith Wharton says beauty is genius of the skin.

DEIRDRE: Did Doctor James say "Take her? She's lonely. She's mad. She's out roaming the streets right now. My going-away present from doctor to patient. I can't mess around with her because of the Hippocratic Oath, but you give her a good boff for me." Is that what the mind butcher said to you? Is that how you spend your sessions? Talking about me? How many other patients has old stud Doctor James fixed you up with? The mother who drinks? Is she another one of your old discards? You are wasting your forty bucks an hour. The two of you. Two Freudian mind fuckers. He tells you all my secrets? The two of you having a bloody good laugh on my account? I thought you and I *shared* Doctor James. Brothers and sisters? Going in to visit our father? Brothers and sisters? Hah!

SCOOPER: Forty dollars an hour?

DEIRDRE: I suddenly understand incest.

SCOOPER: Forty dollars an hour????

DEIRDRE: You have successfully ruined Doctor James for this analysand. I can never go back to him again.

SCOOPER: He charges me fifty dollars an hour.

DEIRDRE: Fifty dollars an hour?

SCOOPER: He charges you forty dollars an hour?

DEIRDRE: Forty.

SCOOPER: Why does he charge me fifty?

DEIRDRE: He charges you fifty?

SCOOPER: Fifty and forty? It doesn't seem fair.

DEIRDRE: He charges me forty because I am his favorite patient.

SCOOPER: Don't say that.

DEIRDRE: Sometimes he doesn't even charge me. Sometimes he says you are so interesting, I should be giving you money just for the privilege of listening to you pour out your heart.

SCOOPER: He doesn't say that.

DEIRDRE: No, he doesn't.

SCOOPER: But he does charge you forty.

DEIRDRE: Forty.

SCOOPER: How many days a week?

DEIRDRE: Five.

SCOOPER: How many years?

DEIRDRE: Eight.

SCOOPER: You must be very sick.

DEIRDRE: How long for you?

SCOOPER: Six.

DEIRDRE: How many days a week?

SCOOPER: The three I see you.

DEIRDRE: Oh, therapy. You're only in therapy.

SCOOPER: I'm in analysis.

DEIRDRE: Three days a week? Gerber's Baby Food analysis. On the other hand, we have me! Five days a week! Depths of my psyche! Sonar waves into my soul! Psychic barium cocktails.

SCOOPER: Wait. You go early in the morning.

DEIRDRE: Gallop straight from my dreams to the couch.

SCOOPER: Oh, I know what you're in.

DEIRDRE: Doctor can't wait to start off his day with a high.

SCOOPER: You're in supportive analysis.

DEIRDRE: Deep classical.

SCOOPER: You're one of those sad neurotics who have to go first thing in the morning just to get enough courage—

DEIRDRE, *holding her ears:* What Beethoven is to the sonata, I am to the couch!

SCOOPER: —just to get through the day.

DEIRDRE: I am *not* in supportive.

SCOOPER: You're one of those cripples who can only take life in twenty-four-hour doses. Then off to daddy.

DEIRDRE: I am very strong.

SCOOPER: When did he say you were strong?

DEIRDRE: You're the one who listens at the door. You tell me.

SCOOPER: He hardly says anything ever to me.

DEIRDRE: To me he gives wonders.

SCOOPER: All I know is I possess enough strength to get through a simple day.

DEIRDRE: To me he tells secrets of living.

SCOOPER: I only need him three days a week.

DEIRDRE: He reads me from the Secret Freud Handbook.

SCOOPER: I don't use him for a crutch.

DEIRDRE: He wants me to be free.

SCOOPER: I don't think Doctor James likes the kind of patient who uses him for a crutch.

DEIRDRE: He says Deirdre, I learn from you!

SCOOPER: He has you first just to get the worst out of the way.

DEIRDRE: It boils down to this.

SCOOPER: He's not helping you if he's charging you charity fees.

DEIRDRE: I am in analysis. You are in therapy. You are going to him for one specific problem. Your girlfriend. Your mother. I am going to him for my whole life. All the fantasies I wasted on you. I had you trapped in this Dostoevskian turmoil. A fellow tormentee. Someone who is my match. Someone who understands. What do I get picked up by? Cuticle despair. Is that why the little baby's going to Doctor James? His little cuticle hurts?

SCOOPER: You're being very hostile.

DEIRDRE: You have discovered the mouth of the River Hostility. You are drowning in the Great Lakes of Hostility.

SCOOPER: Don't say that.

DEIRDRE: Oh, little baby can dish it out. But little baby can't take it. You want to know why I'm spending the best years of my life on Doctor James's couch? And it looks like my sunset years. You want to know the magic event that will clarify everything for you? Little magic key revelations? I hurt someone. Hurt them very badly.

SCOOPER: You don't mean breaking hearts.

DEIRDRE: We both share a relationship of a long nature with a married person. *She lights a cigarette.*

SCOOPER: Of which sex?

DEIRDRE: A married person. This married person sat in a hotel room and told me this person was going back to their mate. Finally. Over. I had trouble hearing because the

ashtray on the table between us started talking to me.
The ashtray was empty because both of us had stopped
smoking. We had met at a SmokEnders clinic and it
made us think we had a great deal in common and we
had both not smoked for a long time now and I felt
proud of that. But now words like Over and Returning
became our vocabularies' main themes and this ashtray
says to me Just because you don't smoke anymore doesn't
mean you have to neglect me. And the ashtray starts
singing in this lovely clear voice the old Jerome Kern
standard "Why Was I Born?" And this person whose
lungs I have helped clear packs a suitcase and calls room
service and orders a pack of cigarettes. Camels. Lucky
Strikes. Anything without a filter. And I knew it was
over. And we sat there a long time. Room service brings
the smokes. A pot of decaffeinated coffee. And the ashtray
suddenly stops singing and says I'll tell you why you were
born. To free yourself. Do it. Use me! I picked up the
ashtray and could see the person all distorted in its glass
base. I brought it down on the side of this person's head.

SCOOPER: Did you kill this person?

DEIRDRE: The person turned to light the cigarette. The match
flew out of my friend's hand and landed on blue pajamas
which I thought were silk but were this incendiary Orlon
and the suitcase burst into flame and I threw the de-caf
coffee on the bed and put out the fire and called room
service to take care of this person with the gash on the
person's head and in a secret way found Doctor James
and have been going to him everyday since that day.

SCOOPER: This person. Was it a man or a woman?

DEIRDRE: It was a man, goddamit. *She picks up an ashtray.*
A man! You're like every other man I ever met in my

life. You come on like this great oral aggressive, but at
heart you're this anal retentive . . .

SCOOPER: I think . . . really wish you would put that down.
I'm not like your friend. I stopped smoking and have not
started up. Put it down. *She puts the ashtray down quietly.*
I saw you in the waiting room. I couldn't look at you
because of the desperation smeared all over your face.
I said Is that what I look like?

DEIRDRE: Then you must have felt some sympathy for me. If
you saw my agony.

SCOOPER: There's no sympathy in a doctor's waiting room.
Only me next. Me next. I picked you up today because
I was sad Doctor James was leaving, crazy because I am
finally leaving with the woman I love after a trillion
years of waiting. I'm losing a close friend, Ted, my old
college roommate. And my mother's body bursts open
and I'm furious at her for not trusting me enough to
tell me two years ago and I see you, beside the books, and
I just wanted to connect to you.

DEIRDRE: E. M. Forster says that. Connect. Only connect.

SCOOPER: Fuck E. M. Forster. I just wanted to sit down and
share.

DEIRDRE: And what did you find out?

SCOOPER: That I'm being overcharged.

DEIRDRE: I'm sorry I said you were only in therapy.

SCOOPER: It's the meanest thing anybody ever said to me.

DEIRDRE: Well, if that's the meanest thing—

SCOOPER: I'd better go. Up to the hospital. Find out what I can
before I'm off. *He picks up his suitcase and stands at the
door.* We'll meet again.

DEIRDRE: You'll be all healthy, living with the world's most
perfect woman. I don't think we'll meet.

SCOOPER: Thank you for the Greene. *He starts to go.*

DEIRDRE: My father lives in New Jersey.

SCOOPER, *pausing:* Recuperating from his death in the Lake
 Placid car crash?

DEIRDRE: He lives in a nursing home. Which is why I asked
 you before if your mother was in a nursing home. If I
 can help in any way. We both share a guilt about the
 way we neglected a parent.

SCOOPER: I haven't neglected anybody . . .

DEIRDRE: It's a very good nursing home. It's a lot but the
 Medicare helps out. My father was in the Mafia. You
 don't have to be Italian to be in the Mafia. He was in
 charge of all the pinball machines in the state of New
 Jersey. Atlantic City. Up through the Jersey shore. I
 didn't mind that. But when I was twenty, I found out
 that he had gone over to drugs and was pushing drugs.
 Fairly large quantities in the same areas where he pre-
 viously had had the pinballs . . . I found that out inadvertently. He kept things from me. Loved that I read
 and was smart. But when I found out about the drugs.
 Heroin. Did I tell you it was heroin? I blew the whistle
 on him. I called the FBI. They arrested him. It was on
 the front pages of lots of papers. Daughter Turns in
 Father. Do you remember me? Sometimes for a while
 after that, people would recognize my face. I wrote a book
 about it.

SCOOPER, *in awe:* You wrote one of *these?*

DEIRDRE: Long before the day of the big paperback sale. Still I
 got an advance you'd call tidy. "Turn-In: The Story of a
 Daughter."

SCOOPER: I don't know it.

DEIRDRE: Talk about neglected. It never took off the way they
 hoped. Out of print. No copies.

SCOOPER: Your father . . . is he . . . has he . . .

DEIRDRE: He went up for a long time. He's out now. He developed this very bad arthritis in prison. And his stomach is gone from taking so many aspirins for the arthritis. I'm hoping one day before he dies we can clear the books. He will lean over and take my hand and say I understand why you did what you did. So I go out there every weekend, sit there, read. Out loud. Wait for that scene. That moment that will clarify all. *A pause.*

SCOOPER: What . . . are you reading to him . . .

DEIRDRE: The South Americans.

SCOOPER: Don't get me started on the South Americans.

DEIRDRE: Jorge Amado.

SCOOPER *takes off his coat:* "The Two Loves of Dona Flor."

DEIRDRE: "Gabriela, Clove and Cinnamon."

DEIRDRE *steps out of a shoe.*

SCOOPER *undoes his tie:* "A Hundred Years of Solitude."

DEIRDRE *steps out of the other shoe:* Marquez is hardly neglected.

SCOOPER *takes off a shoe:* A cult book.

DEIRDRE *unbuttons her blouse:* But not neglected. Overpraised.

SCOOPER *unbuttons his shirt:* But perfect.

DEIRDRE *drawing the shades:* Of its kind. *The room is dark.* But like all cult books ultimately overpraised.

SCOOPER: Think of me as an eclipse.

DEIRDRE: An eclipse?

SCOOPER, *undressing her:* Let me move into your orbit. Let me blot out the vision of your father. Oh God—you poor girl—what you've been through—I'd like to show you how much I care for you— *They are on the couch.*

DEIRDRE: Care for Doctor James, care for our work—

SCOOPER: Care for our meeting—

DEIDRE: Have you ever been to South America?

SCOOPER: No. No. But emotionally I identify with the South Americans.

DEIRDRE: I'd like to put another woman's body between you and the image of that half-rotten peach. That poisoned gauze. Restore the womb to its proper dark place. Do you read Valéry?

SCOOPER: Do I read to Valerie?

DEIRDRE: Paul Valéry.

SCOOPER: I don't read French.

DEIRDRE: I don't either.

SCOOPER: Your first edition of Byron.

DEIRDRE: Shall we read it?

SCOOPER: It's uncut. *She takes a paper knife.* It'll reduce the value. I'll cut just one page. *He takes the paper knife from her. He takes one of the Byron volumes. He slices the page, opens the book carefully and reads:* "But some are dead and some are gone And some are scattered and alone And some are rebels on the hills . . ." *He gives her the book and the knife. She slices open a page and reads.*

DEIRDRE: Ahhh. He says, "Had Orpheus fiddled at the present hour He'd see lions waltzing in the tower."

SCOOPER: The pressure.

DEIRDRE: The sound.

SCOOPER: The pages resist.

DEIRDRE: Gentle. *She cuts another page.*

SCOOPER: Feels good. *He cuts another page.*

DEIRDRE: Firm. *She cuts another page.*

SCOOPER: Slice. *He cuts another page.*

DEIRDRE: The odor.

SCOOPER: The feel.

DEIRDRE: The paper.

SCOOPER: The binding.
DEIRDRE: The print.
SCOOPER: The ink.
DEIRDRE: So neglected.
SCOOPER: So neglected.

*They each cut a page. They drop the books. They embrace
hungrily. Dark. Close shades. Quiet. The phone rings. It rings.*

DEIRDRE: No.
SCOOPER *picks up the phone:* Yes? Valerie! DEIRDRE *turns on
the light.* SCOOPER *holds his shirt in front of him.* How
was New Hampshire? *He signals Deirdre to turn off that
light. Darkness again.* I'm just at a friend's house. The
operation—I don't know—there was a brownout. Chicken
pox? What are you talking about. She has cancer. Bradley
has chicken pox? *He turns on the light. He now has his
shorts and one stocking on.* DEIRDRE *lies on the couch,
the throw on the couch over her, her arms over her eyes.*
They turned you back from the camp? Sophie might have
chicken pox? Kim might have it? They're all home with
you? You drove all the way up to New Hampshire with
them and now they're all back with you? Can't your
sister— *He turns the light off. Blackness.* It's very difficult
to talk right now. Why didn't you give him shots? You
have no right to say that—what are you saying? Our
affair took up so much time that you have neglected your
kids? Stop crying. *He turns the light back on. He is
pacing back and forth. He now has his shirt on.* Chicken
pox is not dangerous. You are not a terrible woman. I
don't care if you've never had chicken pox. *I've* never had
chicken pox. We can still get on the plane. We'll start a

world-wide epidemic of chicken pox. I don't care. I want
us to be off. Don't cry, Val! Val! Valerie! Hi, Ted. Listen,
Ted, we might as well cut the shit—Valerie is not un-
packing from New Hampshire. Those bags are for me.
She is packing for me. Ted, you might as well know.
Valerie and I are going to Haiti tonight. When you get
to your group, you'll find a letter from us. Ted, Valerie
and I—Val, get off the extension. Let me tell him! Valerie,
I'll be right over there to pick you up. Ted, we have been
screwing right under your nose for the past five years.
Valerie, put that phone down. Valerie, it's the only time
we can go. With the doctor. I've met a wonderful person
who'll help us with our books. Valerie? I'll be right over.
Ted. Put Valerie on. Hello? *He hangs up. Pause.* Her kid's
got chicken pox.

DEIRDRE, *so pleased:* Oh. I'm sorry.

SCOOPER: Psychosomatic chicken pox.

DEIRDRE: What a month we can have! New York in August!
You can get into any restaurant. Movies are empty and
cool! Movies! We'll see every movie in town and get icicles
on us from watching—should we see only films adapted
from books and sit in the theater with flashlights and
read along with the movie? Day trips to the beach!
Museums! *She looks out the window.* The pianist comes
out. Is he weeping? No, the pianist is dancing! He is
healed! *She puts on the Chopin again.* When you said
you were reading Rilke, I couldn't believe it. I fell in love
with you at that moment. I can mark my love.

SCOOPER: I just picked up Rilke. I'm not familiar with Rilke.

DEIRDRE: Rilke couldn't write for ten years. But he trusted his
angels would return to him. And they did. That book in
your pocket, "The Duino Elegies." That's the only reason
we're going to Doctor James. To keep ourselves open so

we can recognize our angels when they finally show up.
We have been given a gift!

SCOOPER: She didn't leave him.

DEIRDRE: One day you will write that lady such a thank you
note!

SCOOPER: She promised she'd leave him.

DEIRDRE: And people make promises and people break
promises—

SCOOPER: You know what I blame it all on?

DEIRDRE: Don't blame it on anybody. To be our ages and unattached.

SCOOPER: I never read a book that had a thing to do with my
life. *He stacks books in a pile as tall as he is.*

DEIRDRE: Don't you hear me? *She turns off the music.*

SCOOPER: We're the subsidiary characters in everybody's lives.
That's the joke, the joke of our lives. We spend all our
time babbling to Herr Doktor across the street about ourselves and we don't figure in anyone's life. I bring my life
to Doctor James and we turn my life into a lullaby until
I am as fictional to myself as any one of these books are
to me. *He punches the pile of books and begins ripping
them.* I wish I were blind! And illiterate! I wish I could
rip all the sight out of my head. *He rips a pile of books.*
Were you a nun? Were you an orphan! Is your father
in the Mafia! Are you even in books!

DEIRDRE *throws herself on her books:* Don't rip my books!
Stop it!

SCOOPER *pushes her out of the way. She falls. He destroys lots
of books.*

DEIRDRE: My ankle!

SCOOPER: I want to get all this fiction out of my eyes!

DEIRDRE *picks up the paper knife. She stabs him. He is in such a fury he doesn't even feel it.*

SCOOPER: Throw them all out the window!

SCOOPER *opens the curtains to heave the books through the glass. His shirt is covered with blood.* DEIRDRE *is hysterical.* SCOOPER *stops.*

SCOOPER: There's Doctor James. Coming out of his office.
DEIRDRE, *hopping to the window:* Who's driving the blue Mercedes?
SCOOPER: A woman.
DEIRDRE: Three children.
SCOOPER: They put the luggage in the trunk.
DEIRDRE: He kisses them all.
SCOOPER: He gets in the driver's seat.
DEIRDRE: They drive away.
SCOOPER: Come back.
DEIRDRE: Come back!
SCOOPER: Doctor James, come back!
DEIRDRE: Doctor James, come back!

They press against the glass.

SCOOPER: I see the car.
DEIRDRE: Turning onto Park.
SCOOPER: Doctor James.
DEIRDRE: He's gone.
SCOOPER: Doctor James.
DEIRDRE: He's gone.

They punch each other. They stab each other. They are weeping and hitting and attacking each other. They stop. They gasp for breath.

SCOOPER: Put down that paper knife. I'm bleeding.

DEIRDRE: Oh dear Christ. I stabbed you. I tried to kill you.

SCOOPER: I ruined your apartment. I tried to kill you!

DEIRDRE: What's the last eight years been for? Are you dying? Are you bleeding?

SCOOPER: Is it all for naught? The last six years? All for naught?

DEIRDRE: The last eight years? All for zero? Have to get out to my father. To read to him.

SCOOPER: It can't be. Back to go. The mother.

DEIRDRE: Back to zero. The father.

CURTAIN

ACT TWO

———

A hospital room. Henny sits up in the bed. It's two days after the operation. Her I.V. has been disconnected. In spite of her bandaging, it's the first time she's felt comfortable in years. Scooper is a patient in the hospital. He has a bathrobe on over pajamas. His side is bandaged. His arm is bandaged. He sits in a wheelchair.

SCOOPER: Ma, I'm having a lot of trouble relating to people.

HENNY: Every time I call you, you're reading a book. And they're these books no one ever heard of.

SCOOPER: I'm having trouble with women.

HENNY: Don't you ever read anything by a writer who's alive?

SCOOPER: And you are the key woman in my life. The first woman.

HENNY: Writers write books and then they go on promotion tours on the radio and TV and a person like myself who can't read can at least hear about the person who did the writing.

SCOOPER: I would like to examine in this time we have—

HENNY: But you don't read them unless they sold two copies

and been dead nine hundred years and nobody ever made
a movie out of it or heard of it.

SCOOPER: This relationship in a way, a manner, that might
shed light on future relationships with—

HENNY: My friend, Roberta Schildhauer, has always got her
nose in a book. She wore out her library card. They had
to laminate it, and she never heard of any of the stuff
you read.

SCOOPER *holds his side by his spleen. He makes a sudden
retching noise, but then is quiet.*

HENNY: Is that you?

SCOOPER: I got a crick in my side. *He gets out of the wheelchair.*

HENNY: Why did the nurse come and say "Get back in bed."

SCOOPER: There's other people in the room. She was talking to
them.

HENNY: It sounded like she was talking to you.

SCOOPER: Get back to bed? She was being sexy.

HENNY: What does the nurse look like?

SCOOPER: She's the shortest nurse you ever saw with this great
white cap on her head. It looks like this seagull has made
this rest stop on her head on his way out to the horizon.

HENNY: What do you have on?

SCOOPER: Blue striped seersucker suit. Blue shirt. Blue tie with
red apples on it for the Big Apple so they won't tear down
Grand Old Central.

HENNY: You must look nice. No wonder she's being sexy. I'll
get special attention if the nurses know I got a sexy son.

SCOOPER: Henny, you've been lying to me, to yourself for the
past two years. You're going home in ten or twelve days.
I want to make sure you won't ever lie—

HENNY: I wasn't lying—

SCOOPER: You were sick for two years and couldn't trust me. I called you most every day and saw you at Christmas and on your birthday and in all that time you acted like you were sneaking a thermos of martinis onto the beach for daddy to drink.

HENNY: I was going to tell you—

SCOOPER: Tell me what?

HENNY, *sharply:* Tell you I was frightened. What do you think?

SCOOPER: And you couldn't.

HENNY: I couldn't give you my problems.

SCOOPER: You didn't trust me?

HENNY: I was going to call the priest one day and have him come to the house and confess about the sore down there.

SCOOPER: Sores are not sins. Something in you said I do not trust this man who is my son.

HENNY: Did you put the double lock on my apartment? I don't want those people next door raiding my apartment. Oh, the old witch is finally gone. Let's get the furniture. Let's get the dishes. Wheel out the piano.

SCOOPER: Nobody wants anything in that apartment.

HENNY: You do. I'm leaving things for you. I'm collecting sheets for you. I send the girl to open bank accounts and get electric blankets and electric kettles so when you finally get married you'll be all set. You're the only boy on the block with a hope chest.

SCOOPER: I'm not a boy, Henny. I'm forty years old.

HENNY: Forty? Old? You know what old is? When you look back and say Christ, to be seventy-nine again. Nostalgia for eighty. Even eighty-one. That wasn't so bad. To be that young. To be handsome.

SCOOPER: You haven't seen me in years. You don't even know what I look like.

HENNY: You look like Robert Redford.

SCOOPER: You don't know what Robert Redford looks like.

HENNY: He looks like you.

SCOOPER: Henny—

HENNY: The lucky part is I don't know what I look like either.

SCOOPER: The lucky part is this operation—

HENNY *holds her ears:* Don't talk about the operation!

SCOOPER: It was a success.

HENNY: What was a success?

SCOOPER: They got it. You're okay.

HENNY: Between my legs?

SCOOPER: They put a pessary.

HENNY: They put a pet between my legs?

SCOOPER: A silver disc to hold the uterus.

HENNY: My bladder!—

SCOOPER: You don't know. You make everything up for yourself.

HENNY *reaches out her hands:* I can drink water? It won't burn? I want water.

SCOOPER *gives her the pitcher. She takes it and drinks right out of the pitcher. She falls back.*

SCOOPER: The irony is you're probably in the best health you've ever been in in your life. They said for all the neglect, you had the body of a fifty-two-year-old woman.

HENNY: Well, if they find a fifty-two-year-old soul stuck in a six-thousand-year-old body, we can do a complete switch.

SCOOPER: The good thing about being old—

HENNY: Twenty-five-thousand words or less please.

SCOOPER: The cancer moves slow.

HENNY: Stop harping that word!

SCOOPER: They got it. It's out of you. Hallelujah, Saint Jude.
Maybe Kotex and Saint Jude are the secret of life. The
disease in Fort Bosom is captured. I don't want you leaving this hospital galloping pronto back to the old evasions.
Doing anything to avoid hitting center. Not lying. Just
evading. I'm talking to myself as well as you. If you're
in trouble, you have to tell me.

HENNY: How hot is it in this room? I'm burning up.

SCOOPER: The thermometer here on the window. Eighty-nine
degrees.

HENNY: A miracle. An age I haven't been. Pick a number.
Any number. I've been it. Who cares how hot it is. I'm in
hell and isn't hell supposed to be hot?

SCOOPER: You got yourself in hell all by yourself.

HENNY: And I'll get myself out all by myself.

SCOOPER: Did you show your breast to me—

HENNY: Bosom!

SCOOPER: To stop me from going? I have to know this.

HENNY: Where are you going?

SCOOPER: I was only going away for a few weeks.

HENNY: You going on a trip?

SCOOPER: You had it hidden for two years. Why did you have
to pick that time—

HENNY: You can't leave.

SCOOPER: I canceled the trip. Did you know?

HENNY: I'm sorry such a minor thing as this *bosom* incident
has fouled up your summer plans.

SCOOPER: Cut the dramatics.

HENNY: I'm eighty-three. I won't be around much longer to
screw up your summer vacations. If you write a piece on
"My Summer Vacation," don't forget to send me a copy.

I'm learning Braille with my ass. I'll sit on it and learn all I need to know.

SCOOPER: Did you show me your breast to stop me from going?

HENNY: I hate that word. "Breastbeating." Why do you have to use that word, Breast? Sounds like something a chicken has. I always loved my bosoms. Your father loved my bosoms. Bosom buddies. Bosoms are fun. Bosoms are round. I may not have had good legs, or had the straightest teeth, but did my bosoms get attention at the beach. I couldn't wait for summer. I'm a topless dancer now. Half a topless dancer.

SCOOPER: Did you know I was going away?

HENNY: Where are you going? I don't keep track of your life. Who'd tell me?

SCOOPER: Val. Did she let anything slip?

HENNY: I never talk to Valerie.

SCOOPER: She let something slip about a trip?

HENNY: She and Ted sent flowers.

SCOOPER: That we were going away?

HENNY: I wish they sent candy instead. I could eat that bouquet. The food I'll tell you is not so hot here. But don't have them come visit me. They're good friends to you, but I don't want anybody up here seeing me.

SCOOPER: Believe me, they won't be coming.

HENNY: I wish Jack were here. Where is my Jack?

SCOOPER: So you could kill him again?

HENNY: Your father died because he drank and he was drunk all the time and then he drank even more and then he died.

SCOOPER: So why do you wish such a drunk here by your side?

HENNY: To have a man with me.

SCOOPER: You have me.

HENNY: Like I was saying. Where are those nurses? What do

you think Medicare's paying for? I want a cool white towel. Is it daytime? Nighttime? I'm burning up. My head is so ... Scooper? Are you still in the room? *A pause.*

SCOOPER: I'm here.

HENNY: I was going to tell you but I thought how can I tell him with so many worries so deep on his mind? Don't you think I know you're lonely? You got nobody in your life. Things aren't working out. I don't need optometrists to see all that. And now this. Nurses. Me coming home. Who's going to pay for it?

SCOOPER: The Medicare takes it. Relax. When Jack died and you had that suicide—

HENNY: It wasn't suicide. I reached for the wrong pills. I couldn't see. I thought they were breath fresheners. Life Savers.

SCOOPER: Nobody takes eighty-six Life Savers. Nobody's breath is that bad. Jack dying in one hospital. You suiciding in another. Me racing back and forth to see who'd die first. A five-day race. He went. You survived. When it was all over, the Medicare, for some reason I never followed up on, sent me a rebate of forty-four dollars. I made forty-four bucks off the two of you being in the hospital. Who knows what'll happen this time? Jackpot.

HENNY: How did I get in here so quickly? I thought hospitals had waiting lists. I thought you had to wait weeks to get appointments and beds. Three days ago you come see me and that very day I'm taken here and two days ago I'm operated on. How did we get in so quickly?

SCOOPER: It was an emergency.

HENNY: Pearl Harbor is an emergency. An old lady with female problems is no emergency. You didn't have to panic and carry me out.

SCOOPER: You were in pain. Why would you do that to yourself all these years? Put yourself in solitary confinement.

HENNY: Is there anyone else in the room?

SCOOPER: A lady over there. Asleep. Tubes coming out of her. Another lady was here. I guess being operated.

HENNY: Are they ack-blay?

SCOOPER: Both of them.

HENNY: Couldn't you get me a room with ite-whay people in it?

SCOOPER: You're lucky to have this room.

HENNY: Did you stick me on the charity ward?

SCOOPER: It's no charity ward.

HENNY: Let the nurses know I'm somebody. Tell them I am not run of the mill. Tell them I used to be somebody.

SCOOPER: Who did you used to be?

HENNY: Make up somebody. You're the one who reads the books.

SCOOPER: Why don't you ever tell me the truth?

HENNY: Why don't you ever ask me the truth?

SCOOPER: Why did you try to kill yourself ten years ago?

HENNY: Why aren't you married?

SCOOPER: Why did you get married so late?

HENNY: Who is this Doctor James who got me in here?

SCOOPER: A doctor.

HENNY: What kind of a doctor?

SCOOPER: I don't know. He's. They have to be everything.

HENNY: Who does he look like?

SCOOPER: He looks like—believe it or not—he looks like Jack.

HENNY: My Jack? Your father?

SCOOPER: Same slicked-back hair.

HENNY: Your father. So embarrassed about his curls. I said why God wasted curls on you. He said it was a present from heaven: beautiful brains. Doctor James looks like Jack? I can't wait for him to come in again.

SCOOPER: He won't. He's away.

HENNY: Jack could've had anybody. He had me. Biggest shock of my life when he said, Henny, give a guy a break. Marry me. He could've had any girl.

SCOOPER: What did dad mean when he said "That's what I get for marrying a forty-two-year-old virgin." Why would you scream "I can't help it if I'm a good girl." Why would you scream over and over "I can't help it if I'm not a whore like your other women. I can't help it if I kept it for the man I married."

HENNY: I didn't realize I had given birth to a little cassette recorder.

SCOOPER: What kept you two together?

HENNY: I would've called you Xerox, bought stock in you and sold you.

SCOOPER: What was your life like before you married Jack? Before you had me? I'm almost the age you and Jack were when you met. What was your life like?

HENNY: Life like? Life like? Our life was life-like. You like this Doctor James a lot. I can hear a blush in your voice.

SCOOPER: Did you ever have nightmares? You were thirty-eight, thirty-nine, forty. Alone. Unmarried. Not walking the streets like Jack's other girls.

HENNY: Your father and I went to dances.

SCOOPER: Why did two forty-year-old people get married for the first time?

HENNY: To hold up their pants? To get to the other side of the road? I'll bite. Why did two forty-year-old people get married for the first time? We had money to spend on ourselves. We were lonely. Is that a sin? To be lonely. My father had died. I was alone.

SCOOPER: How lonely were you?

HENNY: I met your father in a bar.

SCOOPER: Did it make you wake up in the middle of the night?

HENNY: We'd do this funny dance. I'd pull my bloomers down like a harem girl. We'd do this Egyptian dance.

SCOOPER: My father. Was he lonely?

HENNY: Why would he be lonely?

SCOOPER: You never asked him?

HENNY: I'm supposed to wake him up in the middle of the night and say to my husband I'm lucky to get "Are you lonely?" He'd thwack me in the head. A man is never lonely. A man on his deathbed can pick up the phone and get a date. A woman's different. I had buck teeth. They should've straightened my teeth while I was under the knife. They should've left my bosoms alone and broken my legs and reset them straight. I had grey hair when I was twenty-seven. Too honest to dye it. I made myself attractive telling jokes and acting the life of the party. Slaving in the kitchen. I was always afraid your father would leave. I was glad when he died. The worries were over. He couldn't leave me.

SCOOPER: Then why did you try to kill yourself?

HENNY: What are you? J. Edgar Hoover? Is this the Warren Commission?

SCOOPER: I'm trying to be honest.

HENNY: You just can't start being honest. You don't walk up to a fella and say Hey, today I'm honest.

SCOOPER: There must be something you want to know about me.

HENNY: I'm proud I never pried.

SCOOPER: You never knew how much money your own husband made.

HENNY: I waited for him to tell me.

SCOOPER: You didn't know how old he was.

HENNY: Not my business to ask.

SCOOPER: Your own husband?

HENNY: There was food on the table. You never went hungry.

SCOOPER: He didn't know how old you were.

HENNY: I was older. He would've left me.

SCOOPER: Two years older! Two years!

HENNY: Do they know here? How old I am?

SCOOPER: Your birthday's on your wrist on a little plastic tag.

HENNY: Take it off. Change the date!

SCOOPER: To what?

HENNY: Anything! Make it even older so they'll say I look swell for a ninety-five-year-old woman.

SCOOPER: You're going to die and I'm not going to know anything about you.

HENNY: You know enough about me.

SCOOPER: How you felt?

HENNY, *angry:* Felt? Felt? You make hats out of felt.

SCOOPER: I'm dying I'm so crazy. If I can straighten things out with you, maybe I can do it with all women—

HENNY: Don't you think I know you're unhappy? Don't you think I know that you know that I'm unhappy? You think I tried to kill myself for fun?

SCOOPER: That's the first time I ever heard you admit you tried to kill yourself. Did it hurt? There. That's a start. That's a start.

HENNY: I told the truth. Did the Red Sea part? I'm this old woman who does not want to live in the past and I have this son who is like living in a time capsule. They call it the past because it's over with, done, passed. Bury him with his copy of "Gone With the Wind."

SCOOPER: You're going to be dead and I'm not going to know you.

HENNY: You put me in hospitals.

SCOOPER: Now? You blame me for this?

HENNY: You put me in hospitals before.

SCOOPER: You were crazy. You needed help.

HENNY: Causing blackouts all the electricity they put in me.

SCOOPER: You needed care.

HENNY: Whole coastlines blacked out because of me.

SCOOPER: No one could help you.

HENNY: Major cities. Industry crippled. Airlines. Television. Looting results because of the electricity they put in me to straighten out my head.

SCOOPER: You wouldn't trust anyone.

HENNY: Lot of good it did.

SCOOPER: You wouldn't listen to anyone. You wouldn't ask anyone anything.

HENNY: Okay. Who's this Doctor James that got me in here? I never heard you mention him before. I could hear the blush in your voice. As a kid you were a blusher. You're older. I bet your skin doesn't blush, but my ear is attuned to voices. I can hear the blush in your voice.

SCOOPER: Who do you think he is?

HENNY: What?

SCOOPER: I'm curious to know who you think he is.

HENNY: Twenty Questions? Don't *you* know? I think he's your—

SCOOPER: Speak up. Come on.

HENNY: I don't want the nurses to hear.

SCOOPER: To hear what?

HENNY: I think he's your boyfriend. Am I right?

SCOOPER, *laughing:* Why do you think he's my boyfriend?

HENNY: My friend, Roberta Schildhauer, saw you at East Sixty-eighth Street where she was doing practical nursing across the street for a very wealthy lady and saw you going in and out of the building across the street. She asked the doorman who you went to visit.

SCOOPER: You don't need to see! You have a little blind person's Mafia.

HENNY: She told the doorman you were her daughter's ex-husband and owed alimony. The doorman said you went to see Doctor Virgil James. Roberta asked me who Doctor Virgil James was. I lied to her. I said Oh, an old college chum. They're scribbling away alumni notes.

SCOOPER: Doctor James is a psychiatrist.

HENNY: I know about those shrinkolas. They're all so cuckoo themselves I'm not surprised that's who you got mixed up with. Just don't let him give you drugs. There's nothing those mind shrinkers like better than getting you deep on the drugs. A man was on the Arlene Francis and the Dick Cavett shows talking how those mind shrinkers had screwed him up.

SCOOPER: He's my doctor.

HENNY: This man says in his book they're all junkies themselves.

SCOOPER: My doctor.

HENNY: Why don't you read nice books like that? Books I hear about on the radio that I could talk to you about. *You* needing a psychiatrist? You'd have to be an ingrate! Everything you got. A nice business.

SCOOPER: I'm selling the business. My share to Ted. All over. Finished. Can't work together anymore.

HENNY: Your best friends. Teddy and Valerie. They love you.

SCOOPER: Friends no more.

HENNY: They told me that. They called at Christmas. It's like a home for you.

SCOOPER: Like a home. I want my own home.

HENNY: Never be lonely with friends like that.

SCOOPER: I have been fucking Valerie for the past five years.

HENNY: They sent me flowers.

SCOOPER: She was going to leave Ted but at the last moment she developed this paralysis of the threshold. *Pause.*

HENNY: You and Valerie?

SCOOPER: That's carved on secret trees all over town.

HENNY: What about you and Doctor James?

SCOOPER: I'm his patient. *She puts her hands over her face.* You'd rather I were homosexual than had to go to a doctor?

HENNY: There's nothing sick in being homosexual.

SCOOPER: But going to a psychiatrist?

HENNY: That's sick. SCOOPER *howls.* I love to hear you laugh. When you laugh, the world's back in place. Laughter!! That's the best medicine! Laughter! Doctors know that'll put them out of business! Laugh, Scooper. *Quiet.* Scooper, are you here? *A pause.* Scooper?

SCOOPER: You've been in bug houses. I've had to put you there myself. I've seen you put in the back of trucks and taken away. You're up there in the Loony Hall of Fame. You have gold stars on your strait jackets. I've seen them.

HENNY: And a lot of good it did me. Psychiatrists. My son.

SCOOPER: Six years ago, your son found himself walking barefoot down Fifth Avenue in the dead of winter carrying a red plastic machine gun. Your son followed a young girl for five blocks because he knew she would be kidnapped and he had to protect her from the aliens who would kill her. Very James Bond. Very Philip Marlowe. Just in the nick of time, your son pulled this girl into a sidestreet to let her know she was protected from those who would do harm to her hair and her skin and her fingernails. She screamed not knowing that your son was her savior. A passer-by heard her scream and grabbed your son. Your son pulled the lit cigarette out of his lips and put it in the Good Samaritan's face. Your son ran down Fifth Avenue to the Gotham Book Mart that sells old books. Your son ran into the bookshop to find a different character for himself. Charles Dickens. Something with an eccentricity he could live with. The police got your son there. Took him to Bellevue. Thanks to Ted and Valerie, your son got transferred to the Psychiatric Institute here in this hospital. Your son's doctor was Doctor James, and he has been my doctor ever since.

HENNY: Did she press charges?

SCOOPER: No. But a few days later I got a book in the hospital. "The Letters of Mozart." She had written inside "I am the girl you attacked. I want you to know I forgive you. Maybe a little contact with Mozart might heal you."

HENNY: I hope you sent her a thank you note.

SCOOPER: She didn't sign it. I had nowhere to send the letter. I loved those letters of Mozart.

HENNY *groans:* He loves the letters of Mozart.

SCOOPER: I said for years I look for the perfect girl. One day I snap. It all goes. I become a mugger. What do I do? I mug Miss Right. Nowhere to find her. I spent my time going after women to love them, to chase them, to hassle them, to talk to them, to touch them, to see them, to smell them, to feel them, to wound them, to heal them, to taste them ...

HENNY: Are you one of those transvestites?

SCOOPER: No, ma.

HENNY: I hear about them on the radio. There's nothing wrong in being a transvestite.

SCOOPER: I'm trying to clear my life out. I don't want to be crazy like you.

HENNY: When you were eight years old, you put on my dress. And my make-up.

SCOOPER: Maybe I was trying to find out who you were.

HENNY: A little Christine Jorgenson. Half man. Half woman. We made a joke. When you were being born we didn't know if we wanted a boy or a girl so we got a little bit of both.

SCOOPER: I have this fantasy that one day you and I will have a scene that will clear everything out between us and I can lay you to rest while you're still alive.

HENNY: Did you have one with your father?

SCOOPER: Yes.

HENNY: Oh no! You couldn't've. He was too busy fighting to share anything. Too busy ripping the tops off beer bottles. Bourbon bottles.

SCOOPER: He had his stroke. I got a cab because that could come quicker than an ambulance.

HENNY: I don't want to hear this.

SCOOPER: He couldn't speak. Left leg couldn't move. Left arm. No voice. We drove up to this hospital. Over the Triborough Bridge. I held him in my arms. "All right, Jack," I said. "All right, dad. Everything is going to be great! Remember when I was a kid, dad, and we'd ride over a bridge and you'd say 'You count all the boats on that side of the bridge, I count 'em on this side, whoever has the most is King for a Day!' Dad, I'll count boats for you. Six. Eight. Nine! You win! You're King for a Day! I love you, Dad." I told him that. I held him. I felt the right side of his body answer me.

HENNY: Then I'll twitch and you can hold me and we'll call it quits.

SCOOPER: Ma, feel these pajamas. Feel this robe. I'm not in a seersucker suit. I'm a patient here. I got stabbed, ma. In the spleen.

HENNY: In the subway! I tell you to ride taxis! I tell you it's dangerous out there—

SCOOPER: No muggers, ma. I tried to hurt somebody again. The words all short-circuited. I didn't mean . . . she didn't mean to.

HENNY: Valerie? Ted stabbed you?

SCOOPER: Deirdre.

HENNY: Deirdre?

SCOOPER: You don't know her.

HENNY: That's what I tell Roberta Schildhauer. You got a million of them.

SCOOPER: Why didn't you trust me? Why didn't you tell me? For two years why didn't you tell me you were standing in front of windows waving statues of impossible saints over you?

HENNY: Where's the spleen?

SCOOPER: I stay away from you because you are all chaos. Your body bursting open. I need my life structured, enclosed. I pick up a book. The page's rectangular shape, obvious but important, *constant* from book to book, dependable, the passion, wisdom, excitement captured in the center of the page tamed by the white margin. I lie on the rectangular couch of Doctor James and yes I become the words on the page. I can face my dreams.

HENNY: Your father and I had that song we'd dance to. "I had a dream, dear, you had one too."

SCOOPER: Ma, I have dreams that you picked me up and used me like a weapon against a strange man.

HENNY: Where's the spleen?

SCOOPER: I feel you holding my feet and my face so close to this strange man and my head is hitting his. My friendships with men are all fucked up. My friendships with women are all fucked up. The doctors say you can't live alone anymore.

HENNY: Doctor James?

SCOOPER: He's away. The surgeon said it.

HENNY: No homes.

SCOOPER: I can't take care of you.

HENNY: Never asked you to.

SCOOPER: Why do you want to stay alive?

HENNY: Did I hear the question right? Why? Why!!!!

SCOOPER: After devoting fifteen solid, very unsolid years to try-
    ing to bump yourself off—

HENNY: They were accidents! Household tragedies!

SCOOPER: Now when it's all over are you trying to hang on?

HENNY: It's not all over. You said they got it.

SCOOPER: They got it so it won't kill you immediately. They
    didn't go into the lymph glands. You couldn't have stood
    up to that. They got rid of the discomfort.

HENNY: How much . . .

SCOOPER: What are you saying?

HENNY: Time.

SCOOPER: He said—

HENNY: Who said?

SCOOPER: The doctor said.

HENNY: I don't want any Doctor James said.

SCOOPER: The surgeon said.

HENNY: Get to it.

SCOOPER: In spite of everything, you were in remarkable health.
    He said the cancer—

HENNY: I hate that word.

SCOOPER: Could take ten years till it got you.

HENNY: Ten years?

SCOOPER: Ten years.

HENNY: Ten years! You gotta be joking: ten more years of this?

SCOOPER: Ten more years of this.

HENNY: I must be an awful burden to you.

SCOOPER: You're an awful burden to me. I want to get to a new

town, a new country, change the name, you over, start all
over again.

HENNY: Ten years.

SCOOPER *very quietly:* Ma. In the drawer of the table to the
right of your bed are your pills. Your sleeping pills. I put
all your belongings into a plastic bag and put them in that
drawer. Ma. You can't live in dignity. You have a chance
right now to die in it.

HENNY: You want me to take the pills?

SCOOPER: I want you to take the pills.

HENNY: Are there enough?

SCOOPER: A lot.

HENNY: We'll do it?

SCOOPER: We'll do it.

HENNY: You won't feel badly?

SCOOPER: I won't feel badly.

HENNY: Give me the pills.

SCOOPER *takes the pills out of her bedside table, looking around
to make sure no one sees him. He gives her the vial.*

SCOOPER: Ma?

HENNY: Are these the pills?

SCOOPER: I loved you.

HENNY: Is this our scene?

SCOOPER: We'll give each other a hold.

HENNY: Don't do that. It hurts.

SCOOPER: Your hand.

HENNY: Where's your hand? *They connect hands.*

SCOOPER: Thank you.

HENNY: Thank you?

SCOOPER: For life. Caring for me.

HENNY: Oh, that.

SCOOPER: We'll forgive each other.

HENNY: You won't get into trouble over this?

SCOOPER: With your history?

HENNY: I don't want you getting into any trouble for this.

SCOOPER: Open your hands. *He pours the pills in.*

HENNY: Give me water. *He pours her water. She drinks.* I'll need lots of water. It feels like a lot there. It's so exciting to drink water again. *She shakes the vial.* You're sure you won't get in trouble for this?

SCOOPER: I'll stay by your side. You'll fall asleep.

HENNY: To drink water and not have it burn.

SCOOPER: I'm by your side.

HENNY: Water shouldn't burn.

SCOOPER: Still. Quiet.

HENNY: 350-2219. That's the butcher. He delivers. If you ever want anything delivered.

SCOOPER: 350-2219.

HENNY: I keep a hundred numbers right up here in my head.

SCOOPER: I loved you.

HENNY: I loved your father.

SCOOPER: Thank you. That's important to know.

HENNY: I love you.

SCOOPER: Goodbye.

HENNY: You sure you'll light a lot of candles for me?

SCOOPER: They'll see the glow in Helena, Montana.

HENNY: When I was a little girl, I dreamed of being a great actress and I would change my name to Helena Montana.

SCOOPER: Your own name is all right.

HENNY: Goodbye.

SCOOPER: Goodbye.

HENNY *flings the pills across the room:* You rotten little shit, do you think they're going to let me bring killer pills in here? These are for my gas. You'd have done it? You'd have let me die?

SCOOPER: Take these pills! *He picks them off the floor.*

HENNY: Nurse! Nurse!

SCOOPER: Quiet. *He turns to the door. He speaks to the nurse.* She's all right. Was dreaming. *A pause. He waits for the nurse to leave. He sits by her bed.* I want you dead.

HENNY: God help me if I get gas in this hospital. *She tosses the empty vial away.*

SCOOPER: What keeps you alive?

HENNY: You. I want to know what happens to you.

SCOOPER: I want to kill you.

HENNY: That interests me.

SCOOPER: I want you to die.

HENNY: That, my God, amazes me.

SCOOPER: Nothing's working out for me.

HENNY, *thrilled:* I know.

SCOOPER: What am I going to do? I put all this time into Valerie.

HENNY: That's what I want to know about.

SCOOPER *sits in his wheelchair:* What am I telling you? You can't help me.

HENNY: I'm not trying to.

SCOOPER: Ma, I'm not a book you sit there passively and keep turning the pages.

HENNY: Oh yes, you are. You're my book. The day the nurse put you in my arms, I looked down at you. This complete stranger had come out of me. That I could produce this stranger. Would you take my breast? Would you drink? Would you live? Would you die? Would you be run over? Would you get polio or crib death or meningitis or be kidnapped? Would you learn? Who would you look like?

You've always come up trumps, Scooper. Just when I'm
about to give up on you and I say I knew what that boy is
all about, out of the blue, I realize you're trying to kill me.
That's so exciting. And to find out about you and Valerie!
You could knock me over. Will she leave? Will she stay
with Ted? How will Ted take it? Can you even keep Valerie? You want me to be open? Here I am. Open. *Silence*.
But you're not ready to be. Poor Scooper.

SCOOPER: I'm not Scooper. My name is James.

HENNY: Now see that. I wondered how long you want to keep
being called Scooper.

SCOOPER: You named me!

HENNY: I beg to differ. You were always scooping sand and
putting it in your bucket. I said "You're like a little ostrich scooping sand for his head." You said "Scooper!"
"Scooper!" You made us call you Scooper. If we wouldn't
call you Scooper, you wouldn't come. It's awful having a
kid with a silly name like Scooper. It could've been worse.
You could've wanted to be called Ostrich. People would
look at me as if actually calling another human being
Scooper was my idea. Not my idea! His idea. Scooper. No
wonder nobody can take you seriously. Or trust you. This
is so interesting. I was wondering when you'd get around
to changing your name back to what we named you.
James! After my father. A wonderful man. James. The
first. You're James the Second.

DEIRDRE *appears in the door. She has a robe over her hospital
gown and hobbles in on crutches.*

DEIRDRE: I called my father.

HENNY: Who's there?

DEIRDRE: I said a man tried to kill me.

HENNY: Who is that?

DEIRDRE: I said it fast so he wouldn't hang up on me. He didn't speak but he didn't hang up. I poured it all out. I told him I was in the hospital and I wouldn't be out to see him for a few days and finally he spoke to me. He said "Give me his name. I will tell certain men to see him."

HENNY: Get out of my room. My son and I are—

DEIRDRE: "You don't touch a hair on the head of my Deirdre of the Sorrows." He said that.

HENNY: Is this for you, Scooper?

SCOOPER: Yes, ma.

DEIRDRE: I said "Poppa, that's a play by John Millington Synge." He said "I named you after that play. Didn't I ever tell you?" He's going to kill you.

HENNY: Girl trouble?

SCOOPER: Yes, ma.

HENNY: Scooper! *She leans forward, concentrating intently, eyes closed shut.*

DEIRDRE: He's going to send people out, find you and kill you for hurting the daughter of the professor. We talked! My father and I *talked*.

HENNY: Say something, Scooper!

SCOOPER: I think you're going to extremes. I'm very happy you and your father—

DEIRDRE *hits the wheels of his chair with her crutches:* Don't even mention him.

SCOOPER: You don't have to operate out of his code.

DEIRDRE: My father and I connected.

SCOOPER: You don't have to kill me to make up for all the years he didn't pay any attention to you.

DEIRDRE: I don't want his name in your mouth!

SCOOPER: You of all people should understand panic and losing control.

DEIRDRE: You did something worse. Worse than hitting me.

SCOOPER: You stabbed me.

HENNY: Stabbed! Scooper, this is wonderful!

DEIRDRE: Worse than making me stab you. Worse than screwing up Doctor James for me.

SCOOPER: In a way we had a wonderful afternoon. I had hoped we'd—

DEIRDRE: We'd what? You had your chance. You had me. You touched me. You dropped me.

SCOOPER: And you're going to have me killed?

DEIRDRE: You made me afraid. I want to find Doctor James. I want him to see you for what you are.

HENNY: Doctor James again! The Mystery Man!

SCOOPER: In a month you can tell him all.

DEIRDRE: Oh, I'll tell him all. He'll throw you out in the gutter if you ever show up there again.

SCOOPER: Tell him whatever you want. It's one way to finish with Doctor James.

DEIRDRE *hits the wheels of his chair with her crutches:* Don't you say one word against him.

SCOOPER: I don't know where he is.

DEIRDRE: How am I going to get through this goddam month?

SCOOPER: I could put an emergency call into the AMA.

DEIRDRE, *rhetorically:* Who said April was the cruelest month?

SCOOPER: T. S. Eliot.

DEIRDRE: August. August. August.

HENNY: I know where he is. *A pause.*

DEIRDRE: Who is this woman?

HENNY: Hi! I'm him. But I don't want to butt in.

SCOOPER: What do you mean? You know where he is.

HENNY: When you went to check me in, we stood out on the sidewalk. Talk about heat. Sidewalks buckling beneath me. This strange hand holding on to me. I don't know where I am.

SCOOPER: What did he say?

HENNY: Don't get on the bed! You're worse than a cat! *Scooper backs off.* Is there such a place as Haiti?

DEIRDRE: Doctor James is in Haiti?

SCOOPER: Are you making this up?

HENNY: No! We were making conversation. I said New York's like a jungle. He said I'm going to the jungle. A big white hotel. Talk about creepy.

SCOOPER: Haiti! I could go there.

DEIRDRE: Haiti. I could go there.

SCOOPER: Talk to him.

DEIRDRE: Explain to him.

SCOOPER: He'd want to see me.

DEIRDRE: He'd weep to see me.

SCOOPER: I have the tickets.

DEIRDRE: I'll call my travel agent.

SCOOPER: I have the reservations at the same hotel. *He takes his wallet out. He fishes out the airline tickets.*

DEIRDRE: Fly down. See him. Fly right back. I could swing that.

SCOOPER: Take one ticket.

DEIRDRE: I don't want anything from you.

SCOOPER: Don't let it go to waste.

DEIRDRE *takes the ticket:* I'll pay you later.

SCOOPER: Fine.

DEIRDRE: I don't want any free rides.

SCOOPER: And none of us will ever get them.

DEIRDRE: He'll help us. He'll help *you.*

SCOOPER: He'll help you.

DEIRDRE: And I'm doomed to travel with you? It's like some plot.

SCOOPER: Shoes like a C.I.A. agent. Not one crease in them. Silently sliding through our lives . . . my God! You don't think—

DEIRDRE: It *is* a plot? You never mentioned to him you were going to Haiti?

SCOOPER: Haiti never came up.

DEIRDRE: And yet he knows. He's planned to drive us crazy all along. And bring us down there. He's arranged all this. Maybe he did it unconsciously. Even a shrink can have a subconscious. Doctor James is sitting under a palm tree. We're face to face. Finally. "So our little odyssey has brought us to the jungle . . ."

SCOOPER: What is he trying to do to us?

DEIRDRE: That devil—

SCOOPER: That evil—

DEIRDRE: Diabolical.

SCOOPER: No. Good.

DEIRDRE: Wonderful.

SCOOPER: See him!

DEIRDRE: Face him! Knock on the door of his hotel room. She'll answer the door. "Oh, hello Mrs. James, may I see the doctor? It's Deirdre."

SCOOPER: "Hi Doctor. It's Scooper."

DEIRDRE: Scooper?

HENNY: Scooper. His name is Scooper. Not my idea.

DEIRDRE: I can't go into the jungle with anyone named Scooper.

HENNY: It's a nickname for James.

DEIRDRE: Your name is James? *Pause.*

SCOOPER: I never made the connection!!!! Doctor James. Me James.

DEIRDRE, *in awe:* You've done it. You have devoured Dr. James. He is in you. The transference is complete. His wisdom has unlocked your wisdom. James. James!!!! How lucky you are. *She turns to go.* Goodbye. *Pause.*

SCOOPER: Jane Bowles is neglected.

DEIRDRE, *stopping—but not turning:* Carson McCullers.

SCOOPER: Joyce Carol Oates.

DEIRDRE, *turning:* How can you say she's neglected? She writes a book a week.

SCOOPER: I never read them.

DEIRDRE: A neglected author is not one you choose to neglect. *She turns to go.*

SCOOPER: Joseph Conrad.

DEIRDRE: "Chance"?

SCOOPER: "Sacred call of life." Page 452.

DEIRDRE: Page 452. "The greatest sin to resist the embrace."

SCOOPER: Are we that couple?

DEIRDRE: I can't. I can't keep starting . . .

SCOOPER: Your father—was he really in the Mafia?

DEIRDRE: He's a librarian.

SCOOPER: What's your truth?

DEIRDRE: Like everyone else's. Sordid, banal—of interest only to myself.

SCOOPER: Tell me one truth.

DEIRDRE: New York really is empty in August. *Pause.*

SCOOPER *stands.* DEIRDRE *motions him not to disturb Henny, who has fallen asleep.* SCOOPER *gestures to go outside. He pushes his wheelchair to the bed.* SCOOPER *and* DEIRDRE *go out.* HENNY *wakes.*

HENNY: James? James? Is she gone? Take my hand, James? *Pause.* O.K. Play the Quiet Man. Hearing the name James over and over, I keep thinking of my father. He was a wonderful man. After he died, I was lost. His dying broke me in about a million pieces but after a while I pasted myself together into some kind of new tea cup and toddled off to Boston for a new drink of water. I loved Boston. They laughed at my New York accent. It made me stand out. I met a man. Don Walker. He was Amish. I said "You must be nuts to love me." He said "No, because I have all my buttons." I said "Which makes you ex-Amish, seeing as how you are not allowed to have buttons." And he said, "Well, you're no great shakes," and I said "Neither are you or you'd still be a Shaker." Believe me, it was funny at the time. We loved each other. I felt my father in heaven was paying attention to me and had sent Don to me as a heavenly present. But Don's Quaker mother who unfortunately was still on this earth would not have her precious ex-Amish son hitched up with a shanty Irish Catholic girl from Manhattan. Even though we were *very* lace curtain. Maybe rayon curtain. But not shanty. Not trash. But only a Quaker girl was good enough for her son. He buckled under. Stopped calling me. Neglected to keep dates. I got the message. I moved my broken tea cup of heart back to New York. Moved into 214 Riverside Drive. Met your father in the lobby. One disappointed person? Meet another disappointed person. Years went by. We got married. To show we could. We stayed together. We had you. And one day I dressed you up and got on the morning train to Boston. I waited outside my old office on Summer Street until Don Walker came out for lunch. I acted like I was just passing by. I wanted it to seem like I had just bumped into him, act casual, show him how great my life was, show off my beautiful child that was not his. And I saw him and I loved him so

much. And after we said hellos and fancy meeting yous
and acted surprised, I picked you up to show him what he
missed and instead I hit him with you. Because he wasn't
your father. Because he hadn't trusted me. Because I
hadn't meant enough to him. I kept hitting him with you,
pushing your face into his, till I realized your nose was
bleeding. He was so shocked. I kept saying "You neglected
me." I kept screaming like some shanty Irish Banshee: "I
loved you." Finally he ran off. I wiped off your face. We
got back on the next train to New York. Your father was
home. He didn't ask why we were late, what we had done.
He read his paper. Had his drinks. Slept. I put you to bed.
I took off all my clothes and stood in front of the mirror.
This body was not good enough. It couldn't get me what I
wanted . . . maybe if . . . maybe . . . I got dressed. Sat by
your bed. Stared and stared at you. This was my prayer.
A better life for you. You woke up. You looked at me. I
want that for you. I want that for you . . . James?

She reaches out for her son.

CURTAIN

ADDITIONAL SCENES IN
BOSOMS AND NEGLECT

———

NOTE: In a production of *Bosoms and Neglect* directed by Larry Arrick and presented at the Perry Street Theatre through the auspices of the New York Theatre Workshop, March 26–April 20, 1986, a number of additional lines and scenes were written into the play. They are reproduced here as played in that production, the cast of which included Richard Kavanaugh, Anne Meara, and April Shawhan.

On page 191, after SCOOPER says, "I am a five A.M. friend," and the stage direction *They looked at each other* appears, the following was inserted:

DEIRDRE: Thank you for telling me about your mother, your father.
SCOOPER: *Life with Father*. Clarence Day.
DIERDRE: I have that. I love books about families. They read to me like science fiction.

The play then proceeded with the next line, SCOOPER's "You don't have any family?"

On page 197, after SCOOPER says, "That breast nursed me. Fed me. My first connection," the following scene occurred:

SCOOPER (continued): Get me off hold! Operator! Operator! *He snaps the wine glass in his hand.* Godammit!!!

DEIRDRE *runs out of the room.*

SCOOPER: I want the recovery room! Okay. Back on hold. If that's the way you want it.

DEIRDRE *returns with a basin of water and bandages. She takes his hand and washes the cut.*

DEIRDRE: "All happy families are alike:" I don't know about you but I find Tolstoi very comforting.
SCOOPER: Are you a nurse?
DEIRDRE, *avoiding the question:* I hope you're not a concert pianist. Don't have to give a concert tonight.
SCOOPER: I'm a analyst.
DEIRDRE: But Doctor James—
SCOOPER: A computer analyst. Don't laugh.
DEIRDRE: I just had this mental image of all these angst-ridden computers jumping up on your couch. Help me! Help me!
SCOOPER: This customer calls me up, falling apart like the fifth floor at Bellevue. And he tells me his secretary wiped out his file. "Calm down," I say. "She probably only switched directories on you. Re-boot the disc. Do a hardware re-boot. Do Control Alternate Delete. Then the AutoExec will reset the default and everything will be there when the spread sheet looks for it." And that's how I speak all day.

DEIRDRE: What does Hanna Arendt say? "Without passport and language we are nothing."

SCOOPER: Well, exactly. I love the way the light streams in your apartment.

DEIRDRE: I said once before I died I'd finally live in a place filled with light.

The play then proceeded with the line beginning "Heat banging its fists against the window . . ." spoken by SCOOPER (page 198).

After DEIRDRE says, "Talk about neglected. It never took off the way they hoped. Out of print. No copies" (page 212), she continues as follows:

The FBI gave me a new identity. After I named names and after I named Papa, our family no longer existed. I no longer had the right to use my family name.

SCOOPER: Deirdre is not your name?

DEIRDRE: No, that's all I kept. Deirdre I kept. But this hair . . . this face . . . this body, all new.

SCOOPER: All new?

DEIRDRE: The FBI set me up here. Helped me get started.

SCOOPER: This is a government bookstore?

DEIRDRE: No. Then they left me on my own. All I had was my books.

SCOOPER: Do you miss your old life? My god, losing everything. You're quite beautiful now. They did . . . whoever, a wonderful job.

DEIRDRE: Do I miss my old life? No, strangely, what I miss . . . the moment I can't lose is the moment I turned my father in. The moment I called.

SCOOPER: You can't do that too often.

DEIRDRE: I know, and now that he's not available, I do the next
best thing.

SCOOPER: Which is?

DEIRDRE: I call up the spouses of authors who mean the world
to me.

SCOOPER: And say what?

DEIRDRE: Look up Norman Mailer. I know how to sow the
seeds.

SCOOPER *looks through the Rolodex.*

SCOOPER: My god, the names here; Saul Bellow. William
Styron.

DEIRDRE: Dial Norman Mailer.

SCOOPER: Brooklyn. 718 area code. SCOOPER *dials the phone.* It's
ringing.

DEIRDRE *takes the phone:* Mrs. Mailer? Mrs. Norman Mailer?
Yes. Could you please give Norman—I mean Mr. Mailer
—a message? Tell him it's Deirdre calling. Tell him
his *book* is ready. Tell him his special order is ready.
The special order. The one he was dying for. *She hangs
up.*

SCOOPER: But you could get him in trouble.

DEIRDRE: Why do you think he's been married so many times?

SCOOPER: You are incredible. Do another one.

DEIRDRE: Spin the Rolodex!

SCOOPER *spins:* Doctorow, E. L.

DEIRDRE: Dial!

SCOOPER *dials:* It's a machine.

DEIRDRE *takes the phone:* Edgar. It's Deirdre waiting for you
again and again and again, Edgar, we can repeat the past.
Yes. Yes. Yes. *She hangs up.*

SCOOPER: I want to try one!

SCOOPER *finds a name and dials.*

SCOOPER: May I speak to Joan Didion? Is this her husband? Yes, Mr. Dunne, I'd like to leave a message. Tell her it's . . . Tell her it's Herman Melville and I want to hear Joan cry out "Omoo" once more. I want to hear her cry out "Typee." Do you have that? "Omoo! Typee!" *He hangs up.* Holy Christ, this is fantastic! I want to call Joyce Carol Oates!

DEIRDRE *takes phone from him:* My father was in the Big House for a long time.

SCOOPER: Is he still in the Big House?

DEIRDRE: He's out now. He developed this very bad arthritis in prison. And his stomach is gone from taking so many aspirins for his arthritis. I'm hoping one day before he dies we can clear the books. He will lean over and take my hand and say I understand why you did what you did. So I go out there every weekend, sit there, read. Out loud. Wait for the scene. That moment that will clarify all. I've gone through James Joyce and Wallace Stevens.

SCOOPER: Does a Mafia Chief understand it?

DEIRDRE: I don't know. I only hope he'll hear the voice underneath. English has the largest vocabulary of any language and perhaps one day I'll come up with the right combination and my father will forgive me for putting him away for ten years in the slammer.

SCOOPER: You put a lot of faith in the language.

DEIRDRE: Yes. Yes, I do. *She throws herself into his arms.*

SCOOPER: What you've been through. I'd like to show you how much I care for you.

DEIRDRE *undoes his tie. Through her tears:* Care for Dr. James. Care for our work.

SCOOPER: What are you reading to your father now?

DEIRDRE *unbuttons his collar button:* The South Americans.

SCOOPER *pulls the tie off his shirt:* Don't get me started on the South Americans.

DEIRDRE: Jorge Amado. *She turns out light.*

SCOOPER *undresses as fast as he can:* "The Two Loves of Doña Flor."

DEIRDRE *opens bed:* "Gabriella Clove and Cinnamon."

The play then proceeded with the line on page 213, when SCOOPER undoes his tie and says, "A Hundred Years of Solitude."

PLUME

THE BEST IN MODERN FICTION

(0452)

- ☐ **BLUE MOVIE by Terry Southern.** Monstrous egos battling enormous libidos. A flying God squad from the Vatican. The small but scrappy principality of Liechtenstein. And of course, the incredible, electric, bizarre and wildly erotic imagination of Terry Southern—make up a hip and hilarious spoof of Hollywood at its finest, funniest and filthiest. (257239—$7.95)

- ☐ **INVISIBLE MENDING by Frederick Busch.** Zimmer's wife Lil says their love is dead. He says it's just tired. Divorcing, he feels as if his whole love life is passing before him—and part of it really is, in the still-sexy form of old flame Rhona Glinsky. Caught between these two women Zimmer proves that opposites still attract, by falling in love again— with both of them. (256798—$6.95)

- ☐ **AT SWIM-TWO BIRDS by Flann O'Brien.** "A fantastic, parodistic stew of drunken banter, journalese, pulp fiction, and Celtic myth. Like Beckett, O'Brien . . . has the gift of the perfect sentence, the art, which they both learned from Joyce, of turning plain language to a lyric pitch."—John Updike (257077—$7.95)*

- ☐ **O, HOW THE WHEEL BECOMES IT! by Anthony Powell.** In this new novel Powell introduces the aging G. F. H. Shadbold, a minor man of letters majoring in media exposure. But his self-satisfied glow is suddenly overshadowed by reappearances from his past, and with a turn of fortune's wheel, his scheming is about to bring him, quite hilariously, low. (257565—$5.95)*

Prices slightly higher in Canada.
*Not available in Canada.

Buy them at your local bookstore or use this convenient coupon for ordering.

NEW AMERICAN LIBRARY
P.O. Box 999, Bergenfield, New Jersey 07621

Please send me the PLUME BOOKS I have checked above. I am enclosing $_____(please add $1.50 to this order to cover postage and handling). Send check or money order—no cash or C.O.D.'s. Prices and numbers are subject to change without notice.

Name_____

Address_____

City_____State_____Zip Code_____

Allow 4-6 weeks for delivery
This offer is subject to withdrawal without notice.

GREAT MODERN CLASSICS

Plume

NOVELS OF GENIUS AND PASSION